Marguerite Duras

Four Plays

Translated by

Barbara Bray

La Musica
[*La Musica Deuxième*]
Eden Cinema
Savannah Bay
India Song

Oberon Books
London • England

English translation first published in 1992 by Oberon Books,
521 Caledonian Road, London, N7 9RH.
Tel: 071 607 3637
Fax: 071 607 3629

ISBN 1 870259 28 9

Typeset by O'Reilly Clark Printing Services, Enfield, London.
Cover design: Lorraine Hodghton. Cover photo: Julio Donoso
Printed by Longdunn Press Limited, Bristol.

Oberon Books Limited

521 Caledonian Road, London N7 England

Publishing Director: James Hogan
Managing Director: Charles Glanville
Associate Editor: Nicholas Dromgoole MA (Oxon), FIChor

Contents

Translating Duras

by Barbara Bray

When in the late 1950's, at Samuel Beckett's suggestion, I directed a production of *The Square* for the BBC Third Programme, with Carol Marsh playing the part of The Girl and Donald Pleasance that of The Man, I was the first person to translate any of Marguerite Duras's work into English. I have translated most of her work ever since. It has been a liberal education.

The Square, which had started life as a novel, was Duras's first venture into writing for the theatre, and an early example of her practice of letting one story or theme migrate back and forth through different genres, taking on, different, sometimes even contradictory, aspects and emphases in its journeyings. This recycling of ideas, far from implying a shortage of inspiration, is one of Duras's many ways of hinting at the relativity of discourse and the inexhaustible richness of things.

The best-known set of Duras variations seems to re-work a more or less autobiographical account of the author's early life, and takes us from *A Dam Against the Pacific* (a novel published in 1950), through *Eden Cinema* (a play, 1977), to *The Lover* (the novel that won the Prix Goncourt in 1984). In every new avatar a constellation of images and emotions, wrought out of a common origin in "fact", is transformed into another kind of imaginative truth, each version expressed in its own particular style.

A Dam Against the Pacific, is, formally, a fairly straightforward, pre-*nouveau roman* narrative, telling in the third person the story of Suzanne's and her brother Joseph's grim yet thrilling adolescence in what was then Indo-China, set against the background of their widowed mother's doomed struggle to save her hard-earned land from the ravages of the sea. But strangeness of setting and plot, together with bracing idiosyncracy of character and angle, make this a far from ordinary novel. *Eden Cinema*, nearly thirty years later, uses roughly the same raw materials, but by modifying them and casting them into Duras's own characteristically fluid dramatic form, gives the kaleidoscope a new twist and the story a multiple perspective. *The Lover*, seven years further on still, appears to re-handle the same basic data, but this time an incandescent concentration is achieved through a first-person naration focussed on the curious initiation into love and life of the "Suzanne" character, now simply "I". Her story seems to flow like the Mekong river of its setting, natural and strong, but in fact Duras is making virtuoso use of formal freedoms won by years of experiment.

Discussions about the autobiographical accuracy of these different tellings of the same story – and there have been many such debates since the worldwide success of *The Lover* – are beside the point. Like any great artist, Marguerite Duras is preoccupied by a group of primordial themes and images which have been slowly secreted from life, and which, ceaselessly explored and elaborated, have gradually built up their own unique and autonomous world. But because of Duras's empathy with human passions and her power to create characters and moments that arrestingly embody them, we feel that the exotic universe she has called into being contains something which is relevant, however deviously, to our own.

But that "something" is pretty disturbing. For Duras's attitude to things is unremittingly subversive: occasionally, as in some of her newspaper articles on controversial topics, it may even seem wilfully perverse. Rash critics have even accused her of condoning child-murder! To explain such apparent provocations and decipher the Durassian code, we need to go back to a short story called *The Boa Constrictor*, first published in 1943. Here the first-person narrator looks back to her adolescence in 1928 in a "French colony", when she deliberately inverted conventional values of good and evil by equating the repulsive but reputedly virtuous Mlle Barbet with all that is baneful and wicked in society, while the murderous yet fascinating snake comes to symbolize all those who boldly reject conformity and stand outside consensus.

Hence Duras's habit of identifying with underdogs, outcasts and even criminals – not because of any morbid love of gore or violence (far from it), but because an outsider's vision may be a revelation, and an unlawful act, perhaps more than any other, can be seen as a dramatic challenge to the intolerably unjust order of things as they are. The Girl in *The Square* is a down-trodden maidservant, The Man an unsuccessful commercial traveller; but together they evoke a picture of the world that is comical as well as tragic – beautiful, and full of wisdom and poetry. In the play *L'Amante Anglaise* (1968), based on a real-life case, the middle-aged childless Claire has murdered her stolid husband's mentally retarded grown-up niece and tried to get rid of the body by cutting it up and dropping the pieces on to trains passing under a railway bridge. The gruesome details of

Claire's act are not realistically contemplated; they are, rather, part of a macabre joke, the bizarre symbol of an inevitable eruption that shatters into fiery fragments the sleeping volcano of Claire's thwarted imagination.

In season and out of season, Duras invokes the Nazi persecution of the Jews and France's killing of Algerians in Paris during the war of independence as symbols of injustice and cruelty that must never be forgotten. Wilful as her ways may seem, she is unflaggingly faithful to her basic vision. Some of her best writing has been done in white-hot anger against official inhumanity, as in a recent tale, an instant classic, called *The Cutter Off of Water*. It tells with chilling simplicity of the fate that befalls a poor illiterate immigrant family when their water is cut off during a heat wave. British privatized water companies please copy.

All very odd and intense. And these two elements – the oddness and the intensity – are perhaps the greatest problems that face the translator of Duras into English. I hope my reference to *The Boa* may help new readers with the oddity: Duras hasn't exactly said, with Milton's Satan, "Evil be thou my Good," but she has declared permanent war on ethical and other stereotypes, and if we remember this we may read her more easily and be able to enjoy her jokes.

Intensity is another matter. French language and culture have a relatively high intensity threshold, while Anglo-Saxons – as the French tend to call English – and American-speakers, dislike taking serious matters too seriously. As the Thurber man puts it: "But Marsha, what do you want to be inscrutable *for*?" So the translator – or at least the translator into English – must be careful, when rendering some of Duras's most powerful moments, to bear in mind that a similar cause may produce a very different effect in another linguistic and cultural context. In order to avoid striking disastrously wrong notes, he or she, while eschewing the timidity that steamrollers everything into blandness, must sometimes dare to transpose boldly.

Duras herself gives translators almost dangerously generous licence. In a message sent to a conference held in Arles in 1987, and hitherto unpublished in English, she warned them against over-emphasizing the importance of meaning as distinct from all the other elements involved. Starting from the principle that all languages are essentially different from one another, so that in translation no exact equivalence is possible, she speaks of a book as being necessarily "transported" rather than translated into another language, and thus becoming in the process a different entity, based on each translator's inevitably *personal* reading of the original text.

She goes further, and recommends a musical approach – one which if necessary *departs from* the sense of the author's text in the interests of fidelity to its sound. She grants her translator the same rights of interpretation as a composer might grant to a musician. To stick too rigidly to meaning is a kind of outmoded academicism, she says, which "works against the freedom of the text, against its natural respiration, its folly...."

In short, against its music. Duras is being typically impetuous here, but what she says about giving her own translators room for manoeuvre applies more generally. When working on a text of any serious value, a translator has two kinds of music to reproduce when possible, and when not, to replace. The first kind of music is that inherent in the language in which the text was written, and which must always be more or less resistant to translation. The more exquisitely right or pithily colloquial a phrase in French, the more unlikely is it to have an exact equivalent in English. Repetitions that please a Gallic ear often grate on a British one. Buts and ands, those necessary signposts in a series of English phrases or sentences, are likely to be omitted in their French counterpart. Add these and the countless other purely linguistic differences together, and you get two entirely contrasting sets of harmonics.

Then, on top of the music of the language comes the music of the writer. In the case of Duras, as the quotation above suggests, this music is of paramount importance, even rivalling that of literal meaning. Just as over her long writing career Duras has evolved a special world made up of her own unmistakable characters and setting, so she has developed her own music – a particular, often incantatory, voice with its individual notation and rules of composition. Yes, and its own "folly" or madness. And these the translator must be careful enough, and sometimes wild enough, to respect in his or her own art. For as Duras said in her message to Arles: "Mistakes about the music are worse than mistakes about the sense".

La Musica
[*La Musica Deuxième*]

This translation was commissioned for performance by the Hampstead Theatre, London. Artistic Director, Jenny Topper

MUSIC

Beethoven's Sonata No. 2 for piano and violoncello in G minor [Op.5, No 2]; first movement [adagio], played by Pablo Casals and Rudolph Serkin.

Duke Ellington's *Black and Tan Fantasy*, 1945 version.

CHARACTERS

SHE: *Anne-Marie Roche*: Thirty-five or so years old. She is very well-dressed and well-groomed, with an elegance that is self-assured, unobtrusive, almost austere, but as though unconscious. It should seem habitual, as though she were always turned out like that.

She has a strength that isn't visible at first sight. It's not that she tries to hide her real character; rather that she's hidden from herself by a model education that is now a thing of the past. But though it is no longer taught formally, there are still women affected by the tradition of that upbringing, handed down from mothers to daughters. Its main feature is a knowledge of men of which women themselves are supposed to be unaware, and which must be concealed from men. A kind of Jesuitry, at once innocent and dangerous, which surrounds such women like a zone of silence.

Anne-Marie Roche has survived what happened between her and Michel Nollet: two years after they left Evreux, she is still there. As conditioned as ever by her upbringing, she is reserved even with him; modest even with him, her lover. She has been taught not to show anything; but we see it all. The irreversible failure of her life is revealed through countless small, almost imperceptible gestures: a wave of the hand, the way she puts her elbows on the table, stands up, sits down, stands up again – all the different ways she has of doing these things; also through the way she expresses violent feelings through words rather than by raising her voice, the way she gets overcome by emotion, the way she makes you think it will be all right, or that perhaps you have got it all wrong. The way she always makes it seem as if some law is sweeping you helplessly towards the unknown. Then just as you think you're going to die if you don't find out what it is, the unknown is revealed.

HE: *Michel Nollet*: Thirty-five or so years old. When they were married, he talked about going away on the very day they moved into their house. And went on talking about it every day from then on. One day he wanted to kill – kill her, his love. He is terrifying, like lightning, like truth, like passion, and yet one loves him like a child, a brother, a lover. He is very handsome, but at once oblivious and fully aware of his good looks, as he might be with a gun or with his own experience. He's not a man it's difficult to know; he's a man it's impossible to know. Behind him stretches a line of dark-skinned men – back to Alexandria or Babylon or the shores of the Sea of Galilee. His name is Michel Nollet – a Parisian name replaces one that is forgotten. He might be a terrific actor if he felt like it. If he didn't feel like it, heaven knows what he'd do: perhaps wander the streets looking at things. We don't know. What we do know is that he might be an actor. He might be an architect. He might be a writer. He might be a Jew. All these are possibilities. What he must be is what he is in *La Musica Deuxième* – the man she knows, a man more dead than alive because she is about to disappear out of his life. He wants her, Anne-Marie Roche. If the whole world isn't given to him by her, he rejects it, chucks it away. He doesn't care about happiness, money, love, women, morals or philosophy. He wants only her, the one who knows for both of them, as the man from Lahore knows for A.M.S., that they are a couple who can dispense with a "love story."

A luxury hotel in a town in Northern France.

The stage represents part of the entrance lounge, itself a segment of a circle made up by the auditorium as a whole.

So it's as if the audience itself were in the lounge.

In the background, a street with grey apartment blocks. Then a revolving door to check the wind that blows from the northern beaches. Nearer still, a corridor leading on one side to an invisible reception desk and on the other to an invisible bar.

We are in the provinces, and although it's only nine o'clock in the evening all the lights are out except for two small gold rectangles: showcases exhibiting French perfumes, scarves or jewellery.

Three steps lead down to the lounge – the level where the action takes place – so that from it there is a kind of low-angle shot on the door and the exterior.

The lounge contains a couple of bridge tables, a number of chairs, a red settee and a hotel-type writing desk: these may act as markers for the actors as they move about.

On either side of the lounge is depicted a large mirror reflecting an unseen central light. There is also a rather wan yellow wall-light in the middle of the corridor leading to reception and bar. When day breaks at the end of the play, this wall-light, together with those illuminating the showcases, fades as the street outside brightens and the Duke Ellington music suddenly fades into the distance, like a train.

Cards, glasses, a carafe of water and some ashtrays left lying on the two bridge tables show that others have lingered here before the people in the play. The uncollected glasses show that the bar has probably closed.

There's a space of three or four yards between the two tables, one of which is closer to the auditorium than the other. Most of the action of the play takes place in the area between the tables and the chairs.

The revolving door turns and MICHEL NOLLET enters. He disappears in the direction of the bar, reappears, then vanishes again in the direction of the reception desk, from which he returns carrying a key, He comes down the steps into the lounge. Glances round unobtrusively, though clearly looking for someone. He looks unhappy. Perhaps he glances at his watch. He's due to make a telephone call. He goes over to the phone, and asks for a Paris number.

He: I'd like to speak to a number in Paris, please. [*Pause*] Four-five four-eight eight-nine two-six. [*Pause*] I'll take it in the lounge. [*Pause*] Room 36. Thank you.

[*He doesn't sit down. He's obviously waiting for ANNE-MARIE ROCHE. But he doesn't look towards the door. And when she comes in she won't be able to see him in his present position*]

[*She comes in. He freezes before we see her, as if he'd recognized her footsteps out in the street. Like him she disappears in the direction of the reception desk*]

[*She comes back holding a key and a telegram. She enters the lounge, goes over to a table, opens the telegram and reads it*]

[*At this moment the phone rings. She looks round and sees him: a dead man standing with his back to her. He turns round. They look at one another. He goes slowly over to the telephone. And now it's she who is standing there, dead. They both seem to stand there dead as the telephone call takes its course*]

Woman's Voice: [*Off, very faint*] Is that you, Michel?

He: Yes. How are you?

Woman's Voice: All right. [*Pause*] Is it over?

He: Yes.

[*Silence*]

Woman's Voice: So?

He: Nothing. [*Pause*] What do you expect me to say?...[*Faint smile*] That's life, as they say...It must always be like this...

[*Silence*]

Woman's Voice: Like what?

He: Well...Difficult...Upsetting...[*He smiles at the conventional words*]

[*Silence*]

Woman's Voice: You will be back tomorrow, Michel?

He: Yes. Eleven-twenty at the Gare Saint-Lazare.

Woman's Voice: I'll be waiting for you at the main entrance. [*Pause. Then with a mixture a uneasiness and impatience*] You will tell me what happened in Evreux, one day, won't you?

He: I shouldn't think so. But who knows? One day, perhaps...

Woman's Voice: Where is she staying?

He: I don't know...in some hotel, I suppose. I don't know which one...

Woman's Voice: Will you show me Evreux one day?

He: [*Laughing a little*] If it means so much to you...See you tomorrow then.

Woman's Voice: See you tomorrow.

[*He replaces the receiver very slowly. Then turns round*]

[*They look at one another*]

[*He speaks to her*]

He: I wanted to say...If there's anything I can do ...

[*Strained smile*]

> ...about the furniture that's in store...I could arrange for it to be sent... Save you the trouble...

She: What furniture? [*She remembers*] Oh, yes...No, thanks. [*Pause*] I don't know what I'm going to do yet...whether I shall keep any of it or not...But thank you...

[*They stand there, lost for words. Perhaps she makes a slight move toward the corridor leading to the bedrooms. He speaks and checks her. She'll stay. The play will exist*]

He: [*Standing up*] Why don't we talk?

She: Why should we talk?

He: No reason... Because we haven't got anything else to do.

[*She makes a face: distaste, bitterness, sadness*]

She: It's over... finished. Nothing was ever more so.

He: [*Hesitates. Then*] We *could* be dead... Or do you include death?

[*He smiles. She does not*]

She: I don't know... Perhaps.

[*He doesn't answer. Silence. She doesn't want to talk, but does so to end the constraint*]

> Thanks for your offer about the furniture. I've thought about it and I don't want it... It would be in the way... But if you'd like to have it...[*Pause. Faint smile*] We don't have to stick to the legal share-out.

He: [*Faint smile*] No — no thanks. [*Thinking of something else*] No, I don't want anything.

[*Pause*]

She: What shall we do about it then?

He: [*Still thinking about something else*] I don't know. Nothing. Leave it where it is...

She: [*Smiling*] All right.

[*Silence*]

He: Would you like a drink?

[*She shrugs as if to say "Why not?" He goes towards the reception desk and disappears for a moment. She is left alone. She is shattered at seeing him again. He comes back*]

He: [*Smiling*] Everyone seems to have gone to bed. Sorry.

She: [*Smiling*] It doesn't matter.

[*She gets up. They don't know what attitude to adopt. They can only exchange platitudes*]

He: [*Trying to seem at ease*] The town's changed beyond recognition, hasn't it?

She: Not all that much, out at La Boissière.

He: No... The development's mostly in the north, where they're building the airport.

She: Yes... It'll be a good thing for them to have an airport. Make an enormous difference to the place.

He: You've been back... to La Boissière?

She: [*Surprised look*] Well, yes. I hadn't been back here since...[*Smiling*] You've just been out there yourself, haven't you?

He: [*Surprised, embarrassed*] How did you know?

She: I thought I saw you up on the hill when I got there...But I wasn't sure...

He: [*Not looking at her*] Yes, I went by the house. [*Embarrassed pause*] I didn't remember the people who bought it being as young as that. Did you?

She: No... It must have changed hands again since... I didn't recognize the two sitting there having dinner...

He: [*Smiling*] No... It felt odd, didn't it? The dining room's still where it used to be... Even the television set...

She: [*Continuing without pause*] They didn't say a word to each other... not a word.. Yes... very odd.

[*Silence*]

He: They finished the block of flats I started... do you remember? On the other side of the tennis courts....

She: Let me see... Oh yes... Did they make a good job of it?

He: Yes... They seem to have stuck to the plans.

[*What can they say? For the last time they try to improvise something to fill the silence*]

He: I ought to have come back sometimes to see how they were getting on... But I didn't... But it isn't too bad.

[*Silence*]

She: Is your work still going well?

He: Not too badly. I've just landed a couple of interesting commissions.

She: Are you still as keen on it as ever?

[*She smiles. She must have been jealous of his work before*]

He: [*Smiling*] As keen as ever. Yes.

She: Good.

He: Thanks. [*Pause*] Are you catching the nine-thirty train tomorrow?

She: No. I'm being called for.

[*Silence*]

He: Do you know, I don't even know where you live... The other day someone asked me how you were and I couldn't tell them.

She: Oh, I don't really live anywhere at the moment... All over the place... Mainly in the north...

He: In the north. Really?

She: Yes... That's how it turned out... I don't mind.

He: [*With a smile that's already affectionate*] You still don't like the South?

She: No.

[*They move to different positions. The import of what they say changes too*]

He: I haven't heard anything about you for two years.

She: Valérie sometimes gives me news of you.

He: [*A slight start of surprise*] Are you seeing her again?

She: Yes... I've changed my mind about her... You can take someone's side without being... unfair... That's irrelevant... It may only be that you're... unconsciously influenced... [*Pause*] I see the Tourniers sometimes too... [*Pause*] That's all, though, I think...

[*These are passing allusions, never clarified, to their shared past*]

He: [*Taking the plunge*] I didn't think you'd come alone... I thought there'd be someone with you.

She: [*Wave of the hand*] No... As you see...[*Pause*] You came alone too...

He: Yes... There didn't seem any point...

She: No...

[*She makes a gesture to convey that it was the same for her. Very faint smiles. First glances. Deep embarrassment... But curiosity gets the better of it*]

[*Silence*]

He: Do you really include death?

[*The tempo very slow at this point. She doesn't answer*]

He said it was more over than death.

She: I said I didn't know.

[*Silence*]

He: [*Suddenly violent*] You know, when you came back from Paris... I was waiting for you at the station... On the platform...

[*She looks at him. He lowers his eyes, stops laughing, doesn't go on... She gets up from her armchair, takes a few steps round the room. He isn't surprised at her moving: at the fact that she can't keep still. While She's standing up he plunges in even further*]

He: [*Violent but polite*] Will you be getting married again?

She: [*Violent too*] What happened at the station?

[*Silence. He hesitates, doesn't say anything. She doesn't press him. Brief sense of other such passages between them in the past*]

She: I'm getting married again in August.

He: In three months' time...

She: Yes, as soon as the decree's made absolute. It's a stupid rule, but what can you do?

He: Yes.

She: [*Letting him have it, but with her usual decorum*] Then we're going away. We're going to live in America. [*Pause*] I want... a quiet life... It's a bit late, I know, even for that... I must hurry to make up for lost time.

[*She smiles. Polite again*]

He: So now you think time doesn't always have to be lost?

She: It's just a manner of speaking... I've never thought about it... Not really.

[*Silence*]

And you — what are *you* going to do?

He: The same as you, more or less. Only I have to stay in France because of my work.

She: Will you be getting married again?

He: I don't know yet.

[*He looks at her, examines her from head to foot. She doesn't see*]

He: [*Almost involuntarily*] You haven't changed.

[*She turns round*]

She: I've got older, I know...

He: I wasn't talking about your face. [*We sense some agitation*] Your face *has* changed a bit.

She: How?

He: Mostly the eyes, I think... The look in your eyes... You used to have a very... mild expression, and when....when anyone looked at you they could almost tell in advance... what you were going to say.

She: [*Stiffly*] How dull.

[*She pretends to laugh*]

He: In the end. The last few months. Yes, it was very dull.

[*Pause*]

She: It's late.

[*Perhaps he hasn't heard*]

He: How strange... Being able to talk like this...

[*He starts to walk towards her, then stops*]

Do you remember those last months?

She: Hell.

He: Yes. Hell.

[*She shuts her eyes, brushes the image away with her hand*]

She: It can only happen so... extremely... once in a life-time, don't you think?

He: What?

[*The answer is really "That kind of love."*]

She: That kind of hell.

He: I suppose not. [*Pause*] Otherwise...

[*Another plunge into emotion, but this time neither of them tries to struggle out of it*]

Otherwise the whole experience ... all that awfulness... is pointless ...

She: No... that's not it... I think you've got it wrong... If it happens again... and I *have* thought about it since... If it does happen again, it's perhaps because one hasn't found another way of...

[*She can't find the words*]

He: [*Finding them*]... of dealing with the... the weariness?

She: [*Eyes lowered*] Yes, I think so. [*Pause*] Don't you?

He: Perhaps I do.

[*Silence. Memories crowd in on them more and more clearly*]

She: [*Trying to remember*] How long did we stay in this hotel before we moved into the house? I can't remember how long it took the workmen to finish... Three months? Six?

He: [*Also trying to remember*] More like three, I think...

[*It was here in this hotel that the most remarkable part of their life together took place. They fall quite silent*]

She: Don't you think it's strange that we remember so little?

He: Certain... times seem clearer than others... but I think that's something to do with what lies behind them... and one doesn't always know what it is.

She: [*Very direct, but as if She were speaking of memory in general, not of theirs in particular*] And there are some times that are absolutely clear.

He: [*The same*] Hell, for instance?

She: Yes, perhaps...

He: The times when you emerge from the tunnel?... The occasional... reconciliation?

She: Yes. [*Trying to cover up the tension by generalising*] You know, if every love affair has its own laws... and I think it does... And if every... couple... has its own fundamental way of doing things... and I do believe that... we ought never to have moved into the house. Settled down like that... We ought to have stayed on here in the hotel.

He: [*Picking up from her*] Lived like that... moved from hotel to hotel... like people hiding?... like...

She: Perhaps.

[*Silence. Muffled explosion. He was going to say "like lovers"*]

Don't you agree?

He: Yes... but there was no reason for us not to behave just like everyone else. We were young, everyone approved of our getting married... Everybody was happy – your family, my family, everyone... We had everything we needed... [*He laughs*] A house, furniture... your fur coat...

[*She laughs too*]

She: It's true. We behaved just like everyone else.

He: But we *were* like everyone else... so there didn't seem any reason not to do the done thing...

She: So in that respect we've ended up in the same place as everyone else...

He: Are you asking me what I think?

She: Perhaps.

He: [*After a pause*] I agree. We've ended up in the same place as the rest. Some get divorced, some don't – it probably doesn't make all that difference...

She: It could just as easily have happened later... [*He doesn't answer*] Don't you think?

He: *What* might have happened later?

She: The...end... Don't you think?

He: We can't tell... we didn't try...

She: We can have some idea...[*Pause*] Anyhow, what does it matter how long something lasts? ... It has to end some time... That's what you have to tell yourself...

He: In that case... [*He smiles*] It's all the same no matter what you do....

She: Yes, of course... But there again...

[*They both fall silent*]

[*Softly*] How stupid...

He: What?

She: All of it [*Checking herself*] I'm sorry, I do it automatically....

He: ...There you go again. There *I* go again.

[*She gives an involuntary start of protest*]

She: Yes... Only...

He: Only now we know the end is inevitable?

[*She doesn't answer*]

He: Isn't that it?

She: Yes. [*Pause*] And no. We know some kind of end is inevitable.

He: [*With difficulty*] *The* end?

She: Yes. The only possible one... But we also know we don't have to shout it from the rooftops... We can dispense with the....[*Little laugh*] the last act.

He: We *were* very young, you know.

She: Yes. And now we can't face all those problems any more... all that worry... We...

He: [*Interrupting*] We have other things to do?

She: Probably.

He: What other things?

She: [*Laughing*] None. But we'll probably set about them differently. [*Pause*] We didn't mind what we did then... At the drop of a hat we'd go in for sleepless nights... scenes... dramas....

[*They both laugh*]

He: Murder.

[*She hesitates, then confesses*]

She: *And* more.

[*A reference to a suicide attempt. He is taken aback. For the first time he realises that she wanted to die*]

He: What!

She: Yes. [*She laughs*] Oh yes!

He: When?

She: [*Looking at him*] When you asked for a divorce. But it wasn't serious... or I wouldn't be here. It was probably sheer blackmail.

[*He is rooted to the spot by what he's just heard*]

He: I didn't know anything about it.

She: [*Quietly*] How could you? Very inconsistent of me, of course, but I wouldn't let them tell you.

He: [*Involuntarily*] How awful...

She: [*Smiling*] Not at all... It's of no importance... The stupid sort of thing everyone does. [*Pause. He doesn't say anything*] Why *would* I have told you?

[*He jumps up. She is scared*]

He: Sorry....

[*She moves away. He too goes over to a corner where it's darker. Huge silence lasting a full minute. Glances. Then she goes over to him*]

She: [*Gently*] Come into the light, Michel.

[*She has used the familiar second person singular*]

[*He follows her into the central part of the set. She tries to change the subject and at the same time to find out more*]

She: Valérie's told me about... her. She's very young, isn't she?

He: Yes.

She: [*Absently*] You don't know *him*... you've never met him.

He: And you love him?

She: [*Suspiciously fast and automatic*] Yes. [*Pause*] So it's turned out all right.

He: Odd. Other people...

She: Yes. It *is* odd...

[*They are both silent. It's getting later and later. Memories, memories...*]

    [*Slowly and painfully*] We ought to go to bed. They're waiting to put out the lights.

He: Let them wait.

[*Long silence*]

She: There's no point in talking like that – we must go to bed.

He: [*It's the first time he's addressed her by name*] Anne-Marie.... it's the last time in our lives...

[*She doesn't answer. Remains seated. They both stay there, unspeaking. Sharp but not arbitrary change of mood. ANNE-MARIE ROCHE suddenly begins*]

She: [*With a touch of bravado*] He was another man. That was the main thing – another man, not you. On one side there was just you, and on the other side there were all the men I would never know. [*Pause*] I think you understand exactly what I mean. [*Pause*] Don't you?

He: Yes.

She: I was sure you would. [*Pause*] I think that made us quits.

He: [*Flatly*] Yes. [*Pause*] It's strange, hearing the truth two years afterwards.

She: It's interesting.

He: I never knew... what happened when you went to Paris... I presume what you told me was a lie...

She: You couldn't have borne the truth. You may think you could, looking back on it now. But you couldn't have.

He: I couldn't bear anything.

She: Not much. [*Pause*] Not anything.

[*Pause*]

He: [*With difficulty*] How did... how did it happen?

She: Oh, what's the point of going into *that*?

He: Why deny ourselves the truth, now?

She: [*After a pause to recollect*] I met him on a bus. [*Pause. Almost reciting*] After that, he waited for me outside my hotel. Once, twice.. the third time I was scared. It was late, outside the hotel, nearly one o'clock in the morning. And... there you are.

[*Pause*]

I'd been to a night-club in Saint-Germain-des-Prés. [*Pause*] But you didn't know about that either, did you?

He: No.

She: I used to go dancing sometimes.. You didn't dance... I missed dancing...I thought I missed it badly.

He: If I *had* liked dancing it wouldn't have made any difference.

She: No, I don't suppose so. [*Pause*] You know, it's terrible being unfaithful for the first time... Appalling. [*Pause*] Yes, the first time, even if it's only a... passing fancy... it's appalling. It's quite wrong to say it doesn't matter.

[*He is silent.*]

I don't suppose infidelity's ever quite so... serious... for a man...

He: Was it because of him you stayed on in Paris?

She: Yes.

He: [*Painfully*] Did you want it to happen, or did it happen in spite of you?

She: I wanted it to happen. I was in despair... I did it to recapture the first moments... the first time... That's all. Like you – to recapture... what nothing can replace...[*Pause*] But of course, when you acquire a taste for that kind of encounter... you get it from someone else...

He: I'm glad you meant it to happen... I don't care about the rest. [*Slowly and with difficulty*] And *did* you recapture those first moments?

She: You always do... even if... at the worst... it's only for an hour... you know that as well as I do... That's why I didn't want to come back... No other reason.

[*Silence. He's still pondering the Paris incident*]

He: One afternoon, a few months before you went to Paris, I... I saw you... you don't know about this... I saw you going by out there...[*He points to the street*] and followed you... It was in the afternoon. I'd left the office to go and have a look at the site, and I saw you go into a cinema...

She: [*Laughing*] Oh yes!

He: [*Laughing too*] I followed you in. They were showing a Western that you'd already seen with me... You were alone. You sat near the front... no one came and joined you... That evening you didn't say anything about it... And I didn't ask any questions... It was in the spring, three years ago... you used to be sad sometimes, already. The next day, after lunch, I asked you if you were going out. You said you weren't, but you did. I followed you again. This time you went to the races – again on your own. I'd never suspected anything like that. [*Pause*] I began to suffer as I'd never suffered before.

[*A silence. She is remembering*]

She: I did do things like that.

He: And do you still?

She: [*Laughing*] Yes.

He: And you still say nothing?

She: Yes.

He: I had you followed every day for a week.

She: And you didn't find anyone?

He: No. But that didn't stop the pain.

[*Pause*]

It was terrible. I was jealous of you yourself... of your self-sufficiency... Once I followed you by car... You were still alone. You were magnificent, driving fast all alone in your car... You drove for about twenty kilometres and then stopped near a wood. You went into the wood and I couldn't see you any more. I hesitated... I almost went and joined you... and then... I came away. That's one of the memories we were talking about just now – the ones that remain quite clear.

She: But that's nothing, nothing at all – I do that sort of thing all the time. [*Pause*] I'd forgotten about that day. [*Pause*] You *ought* to have come and joined me.

He: I was afraid... I thought you'd prefer to be alone.

She: I did, sometimes, as a matter of fact.

He: Don't justify yourself.

She: I'm not.

He: There's no need.... No, I was still rather intrigued... that's all.

She: [*Almost as "before"*] You *are* odd, you know. Why shouldn't someone do things like that?

He: No reason at all. But why say nothing about it?

She: Because there's no point.

He: That's not true.

She: [*Sharply, in the present now*] I've never seen the point in talking about such things. It's really quite extraordinary –

He: [*Insisting*] You could just say, that evening, "Oh, by the way, I went to the cinema this afternoon."

[*She ponders*]

She: No. You don't *do* those things at the beginning of a relationship... And when you *start* doing them it's best not to mention it. It would only be misunderstood.

He: Misunderstood...

She: Some people spend the afternoon weeping when love begins to flag... I go to the races.

[*Silence*]

    [*Very softly*] I want to leave now.

[*He doesn't answer. The return of desire. He stands up, as if he's decided to leave it at that. He goes slowly over to the reception desk. She remains seated*]

He: [*Turning round*] What number?

She: Twenty-eight.

[*She gets up now. He comes back. They're face to face. He holds out her key. She doesn't take it. He puts it down on the table. He says quietly, insincerely*]

He: This is silly – you'll be tired out tomorrow. [*Pause*] You know you need your sleep. What time are you being called for?

She: I don't know exactly... By nine o'clock.

[*They are still facing each other. Pause*]

She: [*Sharply*] What did happen at the station?

He: At the station – I meant to kill you. I'd bought a gun. I was going to kill you when you got off the train.

She: In those circumstances the murderer's usually acquitted. As you knew.

He: It had crossed my mind.

[*Silence. Anger. Despair. They stand perfectly still, frozen*]

She: Why didn't you do it?

He: I can't remember.

She: You're lying.

He: No. I've forgotten.

She: [*Insisting*] Well, remember! You weren't there when I got home.

He: Let me think... Oh yes, I drove to Cabourg. When I got there I threw the revolver into the sea. I thought that was the thing to do [*He laughs*] – I'd read about it somewhere.

She: [*Formidable*] About murder too?

He: Yes. About murder too.

She: [*Confessing*] *I*'d read about adultery in Paris.

He: We were very well-read!

She: Yes.

[*Silence. When She speaks She is over-aggressive*]

So what are we going to do about the furniture?

He: Nothing.

She: Nothing? That's a great help!

He: Yes... I don't know...

[*It's clear they're not thinking of what they're saying*]

He: Did you want it to happen or did it happen by chance?

She: [*At first taken aback*] You asked me that before.

[*He doesn't answer*]

She: [*Finally*] I didn't want it to happen.

He: And you were in despair.

She: The novelty drove out the despair.

He: [*After a long pause*] One Sunday afternoon when you were away... I forget where you'd gone... I went for a stroll through the town and I met a girl... a foreigner just passing through... We went to a hotel. [*Pause*] It was marvellous. I didn't love her... I've never seen her again. But it was marvellous. Natural.

She: Was it necessary?

He: No... why? It was marvellous, but it wasn't necessary. I loved you.

[*She moves away from him*]

She: Any other questions?

[*Suddenly, in the deserted hotel, the ringing of the telephone. The call has been transferred to the lounge. But they don't move. They wait for the ringing to stop. It stops*]

He: You asked if I had any questions.

She: Well... Yes...

He: [*Aggressive*] I couldn't bear you to be unfaithful to me even though I was unfaithful to you. Did you know?

She: Yes. Valérie told me about your affairs.

He: [*As before*] You didn't think I was being very unfair?

She: No. Not unfair.

He: What then?

She: Different. Difficult to begin with, but then easier and easier... to understand... But I couldn't tell you – you wouldn't have accepted it.

He: [*Is this the ultimate confession?*] You know... I still can't bear the thought that you mightn't have wanted it to happen.

[*She doesn't answer. Silence*]

He: Did you hear what I said?

She: Yes.

He: That's why I came. To ask you what it was like.

She: It was the same.

He: Marvellous.

She: Yes. Remember. It was the same. Remember what it was like with the foreign girl – remember it all exactly. It was the same.

He: [*Slowly*] It's impossible.

She: What?

He: To accept it.

She: [*A touch of disingenuousness*] Was it as marvellous as all that? Really?

He: Yes. [*Pause*] Do you understand?

She: No.

He: Any regrets?

She: No. [*Pause*] You say you came to ask me what it was like. You're lying.

He: No... not altogether... I wanted to see you again, too. But I knew there wouldn't be any point.

She: Exactly.

He: I couldn't even come near you without suffering.

[*Pause*]

She: What can we do to stop the... memory... being so painful?

He: Nothing any more, I don't think. The only thing that would have done *me* any good would have been to kill you. And...

[*They look at one another*]

She: And now we're divorced you wouldn't get away with it.

He: I know. [*He laughs*] And even if I want to kill you I don't want to die for it.

[*He approaches her. She draws back.*]

He: Listen — we've still got a little time...

She: [V*ery softly, misinterpreting his meaning*] An hour.

He: Listen — won't you tell me everything that happened? Everything?

She: You're asking me to describe the happiness?

He: Yes.

She: No. You're on the wrong track. *You've* forgotten the foreign girl — how can you expect *me* to remember what happened in Paris?

He: You think I've forgotten?

She: [*Speaking for them both*] Yes.

[*Silence*]

[*With great difficulty, but with inner joy*] It doesn't matter now whether *we* are together or not... But whether we're together or apart... there's no point in making *them* suffer.

[*Only slight emphasis on "them"*]

He: Don't go to America, Anne-Marie. [*He is using "tu" here*]

[*She doesn't answer*]

[*Panic-stricken*] Don't go, Anne-Marie... Don't...[*"Tu" still up to here. Then he reverts to the more formal "vous"*] If you do I'll come and live wherever you live, do you hear? To hell with my work... I'll live in whatever town you live in and plague you until...

She: [*Interrupting*] Until hell starts up again?

[*He comes over. Stands behind her*]

He: To hell with hell. [*Pause*] I don't give a damn for hell, and nor do you. [*Pause*] You don't give a curse. [*Pause. He implores*] Stay in France. Just so there's at least a possibility we might meet, even if it's only by chance... So that it won't be completely impossible. So we'll at least be in the same country... Otherwise... it'll be unbearable.

[*She doesn't answer*]

[*Very quietly; sudden despair*] I'll get in touch and arrange for us to meet... a long way away... in the provinces... No one will know... ever.

[*They're both in a fury against "things as they are"*]

She: [*Shaking her head*] No. Not on purpose... No... If we do meet, let it be by chance, as it was with them — the girl and the man. Never except... never again except by chance...

He: I can't leave you.

She: We've already parted...

He: What if one of us were dying?

She: Not even then. We must do nothing. Find a way to do nothing.

[*It's here that LA MUSICA becomes LA MUSICA DEUXIÈME. It's not an interval. An interlude, rather, in which the action is suspended.*]

[*This is how it should go:*

After the last speech the actors remain as they are for two or three seconds, until the Duke Ellington begins. Then they suddenly stop acting and separate]

[*The light begins to fade*]

[*The actors go to different parts of the stage: He sits down on a chair in a distant corner of the set which is faintly lit to receive him; She stays in the middle of the set, sitting at one of the two tables*]

[*The tables are strewn with glasses, carafes of water, cigarettes*]

[*The light goes very low, down to a half-light. The actors smoke. The smoke of their cigarettes steals over the stage*]

[*The actors are completely at rest, facing the audience*]

[*This repose is a drama in itself, and lasts exactly two full minutes*]

[*Then the light begins to come up again*]

[*The actors put out their cigarettes. They stand up. Go back to the area where the action took place before, near the tables*]

[*The phone rings*]

[*It's the middle of the night now*]

[*MICHEL NOLLET goes slowly over to the telephone.*]

[*she doesn't stir. The WOMAN'S VOICE off is the same one as before. The audience can't hear it*]

Woman's Voice: [*After a pause*] Is that you, Michel?

He: [*After a pause*] Yes...it's me.

Woman's Voice: You needn't have gone to Evreux, Michel. The whole thing could have been finalised in your absence. It suddenly struck me... I was shattered...

He: [S*lowly: clear and unmistakable*] I came to see her.

Woman's Voice: [*Crying*] I knew it...

[*Silence.*]

He: I lied.

Woman's Voice: [*After a pause*] What's going to happen?

He: Nothing. [*Pause*] We've parted.

Woman's Voice: [*After a pause*] Where is she?

He: She's here. We're in the hotel lounge. [*Pause.*] We're in despair.

[S*ilence.*]

Woman's Voice: But why? Why didn't you tell me?

He: Leave it.

Woman's Voice: Is that the hotel you used to live in?

He: Yes. The Hôtel de France. [*Pause*] There it is.

[S*ilence*]

Woman's Voice: Are you still coming back in the morning?

He: Yes. Eleven-twenty, Saint-Lazare. Now please leave it.

Woman's Voice: What about her?

He: She's leaving in the morning too. Someone's coming to fetch her. Now *please*!

Woman's Voice: Have you always lied to me about all this?

He: Yes. About her I've always lied.

Woman's Voice: I suppose she can hear what we're saying.

He: [*Proud, almost arrogant as he speaks about her*] Yes, she can hear everything. Pretending just to stare into space. As ever.

[*Silence*]

[*He slowly replaces the phone*]

[*He turns towards her. They look at one another without speaking. Gaze until they can't do so any longer. Then he sits down with his head in his hands.*]

[*Often, in the course of LA MUSICA DEUXIÈME, he sits like this: his head in his hands or his eyes closed, not wishing to see anything any more.*]

[*She moves very slowly towards him, behind him, stands there a moment, then moves slightly away*]

She: [*Gentle*] So what's been happening to you?

[*He looks up. He doesn't look at her. He speaks. She is about to discover that he is destroyed*]

He: I was offered other jobs here after I left.

I turned them down.

I couldn't bear the place.

For a year I didn't do anything.

Then I didn't have anything left, so I started working again.

In Paris. The suburbs.

[*Pause*]

She: You said you were still keen on your work...

He: Well...In a manner of speaking...But really...no. I still carry on...But it's over [*Silence. He shuts his eyes. Murmurs her name. Her name before they met.*] Anne-Marie Roche.

She: Yes.

[*Silence*]

[*She's about to speak of something they've talked of once and never referred to again. She realises that writing and loving are both ventures into the same unknown, into the same desperate impossibility of knowing. The dialogue here is very slow*]

She: [*Cautious, serious, charming*] That idea you once had...about writing...

He: [*After a pause: slowly*] I never got started.

She: I always hoped you might have...

[*Pause*]

He: No. [*Pause*] I thought you'd forgotten....

She: Oh no...not that...never. [*Pause*] You haven't forgotten either.

He: No.

[*Silence.*]

How long has it been?

She: Since we parted?

He: Yes. Three years?

She: A bit longer. Nearly four.

[*Silence. She looks around.*]

Our home was this hotel.

Room 3.

[*Silence. Then in a kind of rage.*]

I can't understand why we ever went to live in that house.

Of doom.

Of horror.

Or why we stayed in such a dreary hole year after year.

[*She turns on him.*]

It was your job to build houses like that...to build people's unhappiness.

He: Yes.

[*They exchange looks. Her anger abates. Silence. Then she speaks*]

She: At first I didn't do anything, either...and then I too had to start working again.

[*He looks at her. Its the look that's important, not the "conversation." He is still sitting down*]

He: You went back to your old job as an interpreter?

She: Yes. And then I left Paris.

[*Silence. Then a plunge into pain. An aside out of pain*]

He: [*Voicing the unbearable*] You said, "I'm getting married again this summer."

She: [*After a pause*] Yes...Probably...I probably *am* getting married again this summer.

[*Her hand, which was toying with an ashtray, falls back on the table, inert. But the gesture is almost imperceptible*]

[*Silence.*]

She: [*Almost chattily: to change the subject*] As I was saying...I left Paris...and then...it so happened ...[*She smiles*] I found myself in Germany.

He: Really...

She: Yes. In Lübeck. [*Pause*] It's a lovely city...on the Baltic...But we don't plan to stay there...Still it's too soon to talk about that.

He: I suppose you'll go farther away...

She: [*Speaking naturally again*] Yes, I expect so. To America...[*She smiles*] North America. [*Pause*] You know...I always meant to tell you. It's not that I dislike the South...it's just that I can't live there.

He: As bad as that? Not at all?

She: Not at all.

He: And you still don't know why?

She: [*Casually*] No.

He: It's as if you'd said, "It's not that I dislike light...it's just that I can't live in it."

[*Silence. She seems suprised by what he's just said. So are we: the universal celebration of "light," the constant equating of southern climates with "happiness" and "life," is something she doesn't believe in, something she rejects*]

He: [*Gently*] I ask questions and you answer. Like before.

She: Yes.

He: [*After a pause*] You're still the same as ever, it seems... it's in your nature to answer questions, no matter who asks them...[*A flash almost of anger*] even if it's some Tom, Dick or Harry who's got no business poking his nose in your affairs. If anyone asks you a question, you answer.

[*She doesn't answer. Silence. And now the dialogue seem to grow slower, more torn from the depths, like their glances each time they look at one another, see one another again*]

[*A return to the use of Christian names ("tu" instead of "vous" in the French; first on his part, then on hers) is a return to desire*]

He: I thought you [*tu*] wouldn't come, Anne-Marie. I thought I'd never see you again.

She: I hesitated until the day before the hearing. And then I came. Like you [*vous*].

He: No. It's as if *I*'d never been away. I never did go away, Anne-Marie. I'm still there. In that terrible house with you.

She: I did go away. I was thrown out. Insulted.

[*Silence. Then they both laugh*]

All my cases outside, chucked out of the window. But you did drive me to the station.

[*They stop laughing. Silence. There is still something tremendous in the looks they exchange*]

He: I wonder why we didn't kill one another.

She: Anger saved us. We were too furious.

He: The first day without you I was wildly happy...at having got rid of you.

She: Yes. Me too.

[*They smile. Their eyes are no longer on one another's faces or bodies, but on those past events*]

He: Perhaps we're going to kill one another *now*.

She: Perhaps. [*Mildly, casually*] What difference does it make?

He: None.

[*Silence. They look at one another. A new sequence. (They are both back to "vous" until further notice). She reverts to the question he was asking her a little while ago*]

She: So you're getting married again too...

He: Probably, yes...but I'm not quite sure yet. [*Pause. He falls silent, then goes on*] You know...I loved you very much...I really did...And I'm not quite sure yet if I can...if I can...[*He smiles*] do it again.

[*Pause*]

I came to see what you were like...without me...how it was possible, this outrage...what we were like without one another...in this new state.

She: [*After a pause*] Of not being in love any more?

He: No. Of *being* in love.

[*Silence.*]

[*Moment of intense confrontation. Then she confides in him, tells him of her longing*]

She: For some years I've been wanting to have children...I want to live with a man...have a family...a home...I *need* those things...

[*His reply comes after a pause*]

He: Still on about not wasting time.

She: I see *you* still like showing how clever you are, even to me. As if there was any point...As if I didn't know...Yes, I do think time can be wasted. All the more reason not to waste it twice.

[*Silence. She is facing the audience. He is looking at her. She feels his eyes on her and turns round*]

What is it?

He: [*Lovingly*] I'm just looking at you [*vous*]. [*Pause*] You haven't changed.

She: So you said before.

He: Yes.

She: But I *have* changed. [*Pause.*] If I hadn't it would be impossible. [*Pause*] You've changed too.

He: The look in your eyes...[*Pause*] It's the same.

She: What sort of look?

He: [*After a pause*] I don't know.

She: [*Trying to smile*] Unforgettable, no doubt...

He: [*Seriously*] Yes. Very gentle. And fierce. Fierce and very gentle.

[*Pause. He stops looking at her. Remembers*]

[*Slowly and gravely*] It was a paradoxical look...trusting and yet helpless...Always sending out an appeal...even when you were happy.

[*Pause.*]

Even when you were strongest you were sending out an appeal. [*Pause*] As if your strength itself were a disaster. [*Pause*] And you were looking to other people to take it away from you.

[*Silence. She waits, trying to understand*]

She: I don't understand...I don't recognise myself in your description...

He: [*Looking away from her, choosing his words, trying to make himself clear*] You must remember...how the slightest thing hurt you...shattered you...A word somebody said...or a word somebody didn't say...Remember?

She: Yes.

He: Despair was always lurking wherever you were, and you were always ready to throw yourself into it. Remember?

She: Yes.

He: So people told you you couldn't *be* like that, it was a bore, you had to change...be stronger, freer. [*Pause*] And so you...always so eager to please...always... what did you do? Naturally, you tried to change. Just to oblige. [*Pause*] And it was killing us.

[*She laughs*]

She: You're making it up...you always have. You enjoy it. You've always made up my life, all on your own.

He: No. Not always.

[*Silence*]

She: [*Smiling, and they are both using "tu" again*] And you, Michel, do *you* remember?...On the very first day we went to live in the house you talked about leaving. [*Pause*] And it wasn't long before it was every day.

[*No answer, but they exchange a smile of complicity*]

And by the way...[*Smiling*] You say nasty things about me...

He: Who told you that? Valérie?

She: Yes. [*She smiles.*] What *do* you say?

He: I say you were a liar. A hypocrite. [*She laughs*] Heartless. Spiteful. A rotten housekeeper and a lousy cook...Everything.

She: You've told everything?

He: Yes. So as not to forget anything. [*Pause*] And what do you say about me?

She: I say, "He's the sort of man who talked about leaving the day we moved into our house."

[*Silence. (No more "tu" from either of them now) He might get up and walk away from her; speak facing the audience. Whether she stands up or remains seated, she listens with delight*]

He: One afternoon I saw you in the street. [*Pause*] You looked so beautiful I followed you...

You went into a hotel.

I followed you inside.

You went into the bar and ordered a whisky.

The barman kissed your hand.

You sat on a stool.

[*Pause*] You were wearing black.

Yes, it was a whisky he brought you. I noticed it because you never drank whisky at home. You said you didn't like it.

I was in an empty lounge leading into the bar.

There were some curtains.

I remember thinking I'd never seen your legs.

I'd never seen you.

The barman didn't take his eyes off you.

And you laughed together. Several times. Loudly.

I think it was in the second year of our marrage. I'd left the office a bit earlier than usual, and passed you in the street.

She: Bars...yes...I used to be very fond of them...very. I knew barmen in a lot of different places – Houlgate, Cabourg, Honfleur, Orbec, *you* know...They were all more or less in love with me.

And with them I wanted to be as beautiful as on the first day with you. And I was. As beautiful as I wanted.

But I was thinking only of you. You occupied all of my thoughts wherever I went, everywhere. And nothing happened between us any more...except your work. Your architecture.

[*Silence. She smiles*]

He: And do you still go to bars?

She: Yes.

He: And still say nothing about it?

She: That's right. [*She smiles*] What I liked best was the barmen when the hotels were empty. In the summer they didn't have time to talk to me. But in the winter they did. In the middle of the afternoon, when people were in their offices, we talked. They knew lots of women who were like me, who went into bars. We used to talk about that.

He: You didn't have any lovers?

She: No. Would you have preferred it if I had?

He: Yes.

She: But you know, that was out of the question!...With those barmen it was take it or leave it... Either I had an affair with them and lost them, or I left things as they were and kept them, to pass the time with. [*Pause*] I still often go to bars. I know those people. Barmen never have affairs with their customers. Their job is just to be behind the bar so that you can talk to them, for hours if necessary, without repercussions.

He: It felt like a crime...as though I were watching a crime being committed. It was worse than if you'd been unfaithful to me. A worse betrayal than in any bed...It was an act of treachery... You notice the word?...Treachery.

[*She rushes over to him*]

She: [*Alarmed, affectionate*] No, listen, listen...What took place in those bars when we loved one another was just the external narrative of our love...it was nothing. You *were* concerned, but it didn't have anything to do with you. Just as when you took foreign girls to hotels it didn't have anything to do with me.

He: You don't have to tell me anything.

She: I haven't got anything to tell. I didn't go to those hotel bars to upset *you*...it was just something I thought up to amuse *myself,* you see, something I enjoyed so much I sometimes felt as if I'd been to such places before in other lives...caves by the sea...empty cinemas in the North...

[*He doesn't answer. And then he listens. And then he's with her in what she says*]

Mostly, by that time in our relationship, whatever you said it didn't make any difference. You talked all the time about some woman you wanted to get rid of...I mean to say...such nonsense...And while you rambled on like that I used to think about you. Not about what you were saying. About you. What you were saying didn't exist. You droned on like a robot. And I... well, by taking no notice I was able to go on loving you as I did at the beginning.

[*Silence*]

He: [*Using "tu" again*] It isn't entirely true, what you say, Anne-Marie.

She: Not entirely. [*Pause*] Ever.

He: No.

[*She goes a bit nearer to him*]

She: I wasn't interested in you [*vous*] any more in the present...We didn't have a present any more, you [*they both use "tu" till further notice*] and I, Michel. For you our present was foreign girls. For me it was bars...to talk about you. [*Pause*] I remember the light in those places, like in the cinema...Yellow. And all the rest in the dark.

But you know what bars are like.

He: What would we do without them?

She: What indeed.

[*Silence*]

He: Every day, at the end, I wanted to kill you [*tu*].

She: You [*tu*] were quite right. [*Pause.*] It was when I was in Paris that you bought a gun. Idiot.

He: I thought that when you were dead I'd stop suffering.

[*Silence*]

I aimed very carefully.

And I killed you. [*Pause.*] You collapsed at once. I remember the sudden silence. [*Pause.*] And I wasn't suffering any more.

She: And you – what did you do with *yourself?*

He: I've never found out.

[*Silence. The story of the lovers of Evreux becomes a news item, a fiction.*]

She: [*Addressing the audience*] We sacked the cleaning woman. We were ashamed of ourselves...afraid she'd gossip in the town. Everything was filthy, there was nothing in the house to eat. We never spoke to one another without shouting.

He: [*Also addressing the audience*] One night the neighbours called the police. The wanted them to take us to the police station...so as to protect you from me.

[*The pace slackens. Pause*]

She: [*Addressing the audience*] Afterwards we never rang the neighbours up again.

He: Afterwards we never rang anyone up again. [*Pause*] Afterwards we were dead. [*Pause*]

We were found dead.

Together.

Lying on the ground.

She: Yes.

[*Silence. Then suddenly a low cry from him. His face is buried in his hands. Behind his hands his eyes are shut. His face is still destroyed*]

He: I want to be your lover, Anne-Marie.

That's what I want.

To live with you.

Be your lover. Go away with you.

Be cooped up with you in a house.

That's what I want.

Yes. That's what I want.

[*She moves away from him. She can't stay near him while he's in this state. And She talks, faintly, for the sake of talking, about the furniture that's in store... the red herring of the whole story*]

She: About the...the things in store...I really have no use for them now... [*Pause*] You [*"vous" throughout this furniture sequence*] have them...They might do for your children some day....

[*He doesn't look at her. Doesn't hear what she's saying. His face is buried in his hands. She cries out, weeps*]

She: You know what it was, don't you? Crates...heavy ones...Your books...

[*She cries out in order to rouse him from his present state. But there is no answer*]

    [*Shouting*] Have you forgotten you left your books? You sent for them, and then you didn't want them any more...You said you couldn't stand the sight of them...

[*Pause. She is nonplussed by his silence*]

She: There was a piano as well...mine...very neglected...And some garden furniture...some china...and a set of saucepans...

[*Silence. He lifts up his head. Looks at her*]

She: So we'll just leave them?

[*He doesn't answer. Just looks at her*]

She: A pity, though, don't you think?

[*He doesn't answer. They look at each other interminably. Then He speaks*]

He: Come.

[*Both now use "tu" until the end of the play, apart from a few more formal moments. She rushes to him, drops down and sits beside him. But doesn't draw close. A moment of respite. She is at the same time beside herself and calm. They say nothing. Then she speaks, meting out the words, the silences*]

She: I've forgotten what happened between us.

[*Silence*]

    The pain. I've forgotten it.

[*Silence*]

    I can't remember the reason for it any more.

[*Silence*]

Imagine suffering like that... so much... and not being able to remember afterwards... the reasons for it.... [*Pause*]

We shan't love so much now. The others. We shan't love them so much.

He: No.

[*They don't look at one another. Extreme gentleness*]

We're not so strong now, we've lost some of our strength. We've come closer to the end of our lives.

She: Yes.

[*Silence*]

He: I don't think people remember love.

[*Silence*]

She: Perhaps they don't remember pain when it doesn't hurt any more.

[*Silence*]

He: And desire... either they forget it completely, or they remember it completely... As clear as day.

[*Silence. The answer is slow in coming*]

She: I agree with you about desire.

He: How?

She: It's a naked remembering. Or a naked forgetting. Nothing in between.

[*Silence. He stirs. Stands up*]

He: What did you [*tu*] come for, Anne-Marie?

She: To see you [*tu*] again, Michel. Just as you came to see me. And to find out. [*Pause*] Now I know I shall always love you, just as I know you'll always love me. [*Pause*] And I know that for both of us.

He: *I* don't know it...

She: [*Gentle*] No. [*Pause*] You're trying. But you don't know it.

[*Again he utters a stifled cry*]

He: I can't live without you.

Children... I want them to be yours.

Every day.... everything.

Yours.

[*Pause*] We'll stay here.

We won't go back to Paris.

[*Pause. The next exchange echoes the words of a popular song*]

She: You're saying what I used to say.

He: That we'd love one another for ever.

She: Yes. All our lives long.

[*Pause*]

He: Tell me... this play-acting, these marriages and divorces... if they're not to be pointless... what will they be *for?* Just to pass the time that's left?

She: To while it away perhaps. Beguile it... To beguile something... I don't really know what... I don't know [*Pause*]

I don't think it's anything to do with feelings. It's something else... it belongs to another sphere... to the mind, perhaps? I don't know.

[*They gaze at each other immoderately. And she suddenly scrutinises him in detail – his body, his face. She moves closer and closer to Him, but when she is almost about to touch him she stops. And he, suddenly carried away, takes her in his arms, then lets her go. Silence*]

She: Why didn't you kill me when I got off the train?

He: I can't remember.

I forgot.

Maybe I forgot...

I saw you and I forgot.

I'd never killed anything... I didn't know how. That came into it too. And it's difficult, when you come to the point...

And then, carrying a gun, ready to kill you... when I saw you I thought I didn't love you any more. And there wasn't any point in killing you if I didn't love you any more...

She: I saw you on the platform. And when I got off the train you ran away. You came home the next day. [*Pause*] We didn't speak. [*Pause*] Sometimes I feel utterly disgusted with you and with myself.

He: Now...

She: Yes. [*Pause*] It'll soon be time for us to part.

[*Silence. He goes towards the back of the stage. Stays there. Beyond the windows the light begins to brighten*]

She: It was no use our talking like that... it'll only bring sadness later.

[*Pause*]

He: Nothing wrong with sadness.

[*Silence. In it he lights a cigarette – the last in the play. The daylight gets stronger. Some of the lights on the stage go out*]

He: Speak to me.

[*She does so. To make the time go by*]

She: Before I met you I knew nothing about the passion one could have for a man one didn't know... suddenly....to have his body next to yours.

[*It's difficult for her to find the words. She's sitting facing the audience. Calm and beside herself at the same time*]

[*Pause*]

In someone else, anyone, I thought there would be something of our love, yours and mine, that had got lost, and that I could find again like that, through anyone, just through the warmth of the skin the first time.

[*Silence. He has come quite close now*]

He: Go on. Keep on talking to me.

[*Silence*]

She: I went to Paris to make you come there too. [*Pause*] I meant to ring you up from Paris, ask you to come and spend a night with me, one last time.

[*Silence. The time is measured out as by a gong*]

I already thought a lot about dying at that point in our relationship. [*Pause*]

I was sitting in the hotel lounge wondering how to ask you... how to talk to you again.

And he came in. I can't remember if he sat at the bar first... I don't think so. He came straight over, spoke to me right away.

He sat down at my table.

Very soon it was too late.

[*Pause. Silence. Gong*]

He asked if I was waiting for someone.

I said yes, I was.

I was waiting for my lover..

He said yes, it was obvious. [*Pause*]

We left.

It was in the afternoon, as always in such cases. It was a lovely day.

I forgot about you [*vous*].

[*Silence. Pause. Gong*]

He: You [*vous*] were wearing that grey dress... the kind respectable women wear... to avoid falling into the traps we set.

[*Pause*]

She: He was the sort of man who liked false positions, who preferred other men's wives to women who were free. That suited me.

[*Pause*]

It lasted two days... Night.... day.... A kind of madness.... terror.... crime....[*Pause*]

You [*vous*] vanished out of my life.

[*It is getting lighter and lighter. Silence*]

And then one morning I couldn't understand why I was there, with him, in that room.

[*Silence*]

I started to phone you [*vous*]. You weren't there. I kept trying all afternoon.

Your office said you hadn't been in for three days.

I sent you a telegram.

I came back on the evening train.

Where were you?

[*Pause. He moves away from her*]

He: Cooped up at home. I didn't go away because I'd got the telegram.

[*Very long silence. He walks to the back of the stage, stops, comes back towards the auditorium, stops, begins to walk upstage, then halts with his back to the audience. Then he comes back to the table, looks down at the floor and speaks very slowly ("tu" throughout)*]

He: I saw you one other time.

At home.

In your room.

At night.

You were naked.

With make-up on and naked.

You were looking at yourself in a mirror. Very close.

You were crying.

[*Pause*]

I didn't realise to begin with it was me you were talking about.

At first I thought you'd been drinking.

And then that you'd gone mad.

And then you suddenly spoke my name.

You were speaking very quietly and it was difficult to catch all you said.

I listened hard, trying not to be afraid, and I managed to make it out.

[*Pause*]

Then I realised that what you were saying was quite coherent, and terrible.

Without beginning or end.

[*Silence. Long enough to mark a break with the mode of what's just been said*]

She: I was telling him that one day he might touch me again for the first time.

I was saying:

To take me.

Carry me away.

And that during the time we had left to live we must try to outface death.

[*Very long silence. Thirty seconds of immobility*]

He: You [*tu*] must go.

[*Silence*]

[*It almost looks as if she isn't going to get up. But she does. She gets up*]

He: Don't forget anything. [*Pause*] Your bag.

[*She picks up her bag. But still waits*]

He: [*Very gently*] Go.

[*She goes. The music begins as she starts to move. They haven't looked at one another. He stays there alone, motionless. She walks through the lobby. Goes out through the revolving door. As soon as she's disappeared, darkness*]

Eden Cinema

Swamps + Dykes + water
symbolism/

Characters

'The' Mother

⟶ THE MOTHER

her role?

SUZANNE

JOSEPH

MR JO

THE CORPORAL

Incest?

Marxian reading - responsibility, etc.

Part One

The stage is a large empty space surrounding another, rectangular, space. The rectangular space represents a bungalow, furnished with chairs and tables of a Colonial type. Very ordinary, very worn, very poverty-stricken furniture.

The empty space around the bungalow is the plain of Kam, in Upper Cambodia, between Siam and the sea.

Behind the bungalow there should be an area of light, representing the road used by hunters, which runs alongside the mountains of Siam.

It is a simple, large, decor, allowing the actors to move around freely and easily.

THE MOTHER, SUZANNE, JOSEPH and THE CORPORAL come on, in front of the rectangular space.

The MOTHER sits on a low chair and the others group themselves around her. They all freeze and remain immobile, facing the audience, for perhaps thirty seconds while music is played.

Then they talk of THE MOTHER, her past, her life. Of the love she inspired.

The MOTHER remains motionless in her chair, expressionless, as if turned to stone, distant, separate - as is the stage - from her own story.

The others touch her, stroke her arms, kiss her hands. She remains passive: what she represents in the play goes far beyond what she is and far beyond her own responsibility.

Everything that can be said in the play is said by SUZANNE and JOSEPH. The MOTHER - the subject of the story - never speaks directly about herself.

[Music]

Joseph: Our mother was born in the North of France, between the mining country and the sea. She was born and raised in the endless plains of Northern Europe. More than a hundred years ago now.

[Music]

Suzanne: It's the year 1924. The purchase of the concession swallowed up every penny our mother had put in the savings bank in Saigon over ten years.

Joseph: The concession was a big one; four hundred acres, on the Western plain of Cambodia, beside the Elephant mountains, close to Siam.

Suzanne: The first year the mother built the bungalow. And started to farm half of the land.

The Mother: [*Speaking mechanically, as if unaware that she's speaking*] The July tides come up over the plain and drown the harvest.

Suzanne: [*As if reading*] Half her savings were left. [*Pause*] She started again.

The Mother: [*Idem*] The July tides come up over the plain again and drown the harvest.

[*Music*]

Suzanne: The mother faces the facts: Her concession was unworkable. She had bought four hundred acres of salt marsh. She had thrown her savings into the waters of the Pacific.

[*Music*]

[*SUZANNE and JOSEPH look at the MOTHER, so that their backs are to us and only the MOTHER is facing us. They put their arm around her as if she was suffering. The MOTHER, still far away, listens to the strange story being told by her children. Her own story*]

Joseph: [*Lovingly, sweetly*] She didn't know. Didn't know anything.

The Mother: It's true, I knew nothing.

Suzanne: She emerged from the darkness of the Eden Cinema not knowing anything. Not knowing anything about the great vampire of colonialism. About the fundamental injustice that reigns over the world's poor.

[*Music*]

Joseph: [*With great tenderness*] She found out too late.

Suzanne: [*Smiling*] She never found out.

The Mother: [*Smiling*] No, I never did.

Joseph: [*Reciting flatly, as if reading out some unintelligible decree*] To get a fertile concession, then, in French Indochina, you had to pay twice.

[*Pause*]

Once, openly, to the Colonial Authorities.
And then again, under the counter, to the officials of the Land Commission.

[*Silence*]

The Mother: Nothing would grow in the plain.The plain didn't exist. It was part of the Pacific. It was salt water; a plain of salt water.

[*Pause*]

You couldn't tell where the Pacific began, or where the plain ended, between the sea and the sky. It was sold. And it was bought.

[*Music*]

Joseph: The whites who stayed on in the plain made a living by smuggling opium and Pernod. Some were dead. Others had been repatriated. She, she knew nothing about all that.

The Mother: No, I knew nothing about all that.

Suzanne: So the mother had nothing left. Nothing but her widow's pension and her teacher's pension from the Colonial Service.

[*They turn to the MOTHER*]

So, what did she do?

[*They smile at the MOTHER: she looks at them and waits for a reply*].

Joseph: As she couldn't move men, she attacked the tides of the Pacific.

[*Loud music, very loud*]

[*Silent, rapturous laughter from the two children (What remains to be told is above all the story of the mother's folly. The injustice of which she was the victim is taken for granted.)*]

[*The laughter stops. Close attention is paid to the terrible story*]

Suzanne: She mortgages her bungalow. She sells her furniture. And then, she builds sea-walls to hold back the tides of the Pacific Ocean.

[*Music at some length*]

Joseph: The sea-walls consisted of piled-up sand and wood. They should have held out for a century. She was sure they would. Her method was the best.

[*Music*]

Suzanne: The peasants were just as hopeful as she was. The children dying of hunger, the harvests burned by salt, no, that couldn't go on for ever. They believed her.

[*Music*]

The children would die no longer. There would be no more hunger. No more cholera.

[*Music*]

Joseph: The work began in the dry season. It took three months. The mother went out with the peasants at dawn and came back at nightfall.

[*Music at some length, full and strong like hope itself. Then fading away*]

The Mother: [*Idem*] Then with the high tides the sea came up and attacked the plain. The sea-walls weren't strong enough. In one night they were swept away.

[*The MOTHER has been listening to her own voice, trying to remember*]

Joseph: Many of the peasants went away, on junks, to other parts of the Pacific.

Suzanne: The rest remained in the plain. So the children went on dying. No one blamed the mother for having hoped.

[*Music*]

[*SUZANNE closes her eyes*]

The children went back to the mud of the rice fields, to the land of the wild mountain mangoes.

[*They get up. Remain standing. The MOTHER gets up too - as if obeying: remains standing near her children*]

[*Music*]

It is the year 1931. I'm sixteen. Joseph is nineteen. We still have the Corporal. He's deaf. We've stopped paying his wages. He stays. He loves the mother very much.

Joseph: The place is called Prey-Nop. The name's on the Ordinance Survey maps. Prey-Nop. A village of forty huts. Eighty kilometers from Kampot, the last white outpost between there and Siam. Kampot.

[*Music*]

Suzanne: The sea is not so far. Thirty kilometers away from the gulf of Siam. There are islands; and on the islands fishing villages. The forest skirts the sea and the road. It has overflowed onto the islands. It is full of danger. It looms up in front of the bungalow every evening, in front of Joseph, my little brother, who hunts tigers. Our mother is afraid.

[*Music*]

Joseph: It's there that we were young. There that the mother lived her greatest hope. There she died.

[*Music. Silence*]

[*They all get up. The MOTHER and the children, and the CORPORAL. Slowly, in time with the music, they separate and walk towards the rectangular space*]

[*The children go in one direction. The CORPORAL in another. The MOTHER remains alone in front of the rectangular space. The music is fading all the while. She waits motionless for the sound effects to emerge: the noises of night and the plain*]

[*Then, children's cries, laughter, dogs barking, drums. The crack of a whip. And JOSEPH shouting through the noises of the plain. Then the rectangular space lights up with a white light and the MOTHER is released and goes into the light, alone, adult. She walks to and fro and then leans against one of the posts supporting the bungalow. She looks towards where the horse should be. From the other direction come SUZANNE and the CORPORAL who also stop and look towards where the horse should be*]

Suzanne's Voice: It was a week since we'd bought the horse and cart, and Joseph had been using it to drive the peasants from Prey-Nop to Réam and back.

[*SUZANNE, from a distance, turns towards the MOTHER*]

I remember her that evening: she is wearing her red silk dress, worn threadbare over the breasts. When she washes it she goes to bed and sleeps till it is dry. She is barefoot. She looks at the horse. She starts to cry. [*Pause*] She weeps.

Joseph: The horse didn't move. I dragged it over the rice field. It tried to eat, then gave up. They'd lied to us about its age. The sun was sinking. I knew the mother was watching the horse.

Suzanne's Voice: She was already very ill. She couldn't speak now without screaming. Sometimes she'd go into a coma that lasted several hours. Out of fury, the doctor said. Since the sea-walls collapsed.

Joseph: I too see the mother.

[*Pause*]

She is going to get a blanket and a rice cake and give them to the horse.

[*We see what is being described enacted: the MOTHER goes out with the blanket and the rice*]

[*Silence*]

Joseph: She shouts that the horse is dying. That it's spent its life dragging great logs from the forest to the plain. She says it's like her. It wants to die. It's dead.

[*The MOTHER drops the blanket and the rice. Stands still. Then crosses the rectangular space, sits down in a wicker chair, looks out. SUZANNE reappears near the bungalow. Looks at the MOTHER. Then her attention wanders, she sits down on the ground, idle. Music. JOSEPH comes up to her*]

Suzanne's Voice: Night falls quickly. It always frightens me. Before dark, we bathe in the river, Joseph and I. Joseph makes me go into the water.

[*Pause*]

I'm frightened. The river comes down from the mountain.

In the rainy season drowned animals come down with the current, birds, musk-rats, deer. Once, a tiger.

[*Pause*]

Joseph plays with the children of Prey-Nop. He sits them on his shoulders and swims.

In the distance the mother shouts.

[*We hear other cries as well as the MOTHER's. Then they all die away*]

Joseph: She wears herself out shouting.

Then she doesn't shout so much.

Then she doesn't shout at all.

Suzanne's Voice: Then the sun goes down behind the mountains. The peasants light fires to keep off the tigers. The children go into the huts.

[*Pause*]

I remember it: the smell of fire rising up out of all the plain. It's everywhere. Under the sky the road, white, with dust. On the mountainside, the green squares of Chinese pepper-trees. Above them the haze from the fires. The jungle. And then the sky.

[*Music*]

Suzanne: Already we were thinking of leaving the mother. Of leaving the plain.

[*Sounds from the plain*]

Joseph: Leaving the sea breeze, the smell of the islands, the sour smell of fish pickling in brine, the smell of the marshes, the smell of the fires.

[*Distant drums: sounds of the plain*]

Suzanne: Already we'd begun to think it would be better if she died.

[*JOSEPH and SUZANNE, as children, come back*]

[*Silence*]

[*No music*]

[*Only the noises of the plain. The light fades*]

[*A multitude of children's shouts and laughter*]

[*SUZANNE and JOSEPH go into the bungalow*]

[*Disappear inside*]

[*Reappear. SUZANNE comes from the veranda*]

[*She starts up a gramophone*]

[*JOSEPH comes back with a gun. Sits down and cleans it. Tests an acetylene lamp, his hunting lamp. SUZANNE watches him. Looks out on to the plain. The record she's put on is the play's theme-song: the waltz from the Eden Cinema - as if their lives still revolved around it*]

[*The MOTHER comes and goes*]

[*Lays the table: two plates, the children's*]

[*Brings the steaming food to the table. The children look at it with disgust. The MOTHER looks at the children. The CORPORAL comes in with hot rice, puts it on the table : then sits in a corner and looks at the MOTHER*]

[*Nobody eats*]

Then Joseph suggested we all go to Réam to cheer ourselves after the death of the horse.

[*Slowly they get ready to go to Réam*]

[*The MOTHER does her hair up in a bun*]

[*SUZANNE, JOSEPH and the MOTHER put shoes on*]

[*The CORPORAL goes out and comes back with a watering-can*]

[*Music throughout these preparations*]

Suzanne's Voice: Réam was the port at the end of the road, used by
coastal traffic taking pickled fish and pepper to Bangkok. On their
return voyage the boats smuggled in Pernod and opium.

Joseph: There was a sort of Bar at Réam. There was dancing there in
the evenings. And sometimes there were sailors on shore leave,
Merchant Navy officers, and white prostitutes who went back and
forth between Siam and Indochina.

[*Distant music*]

[*They go out, one after the other, through the back of the house*]

[*Music increasingly insistent*]

[*The light fades after they leave the bungalow. The bungalow is left in
darkness*]

[*Then the music fades as a mauve light fades up the front of the stage*]

[*And they reappear*]

[*The four of them together, walking round the stage as a whole in time
to the waltz. They smile. They walk together, or, if preferred, they dance
as they walk towards Réam, all equally young and full of excitement*]

[*Violent music*]

[*They have fallen out of step. They dance, move apart, come together,
freely, in different patterns. The MOTHER and the CORPORAL are in
time with one another. They turn off, disappear, come back. All of them
are deeply childlike. The most obvious thing about them is their
pleasure. As they walk, SUZANNE'S voice speaks*]

Suzanne's Voice: Ah! The road between Réam and the sea. How
beautiful it seemed to me.

[*Pause*]

It had been built by prisoners. Chained together. But how
beautiful it seemed to me. It was the road by which we'd leave
the mother. By which we'd go away, Joseph and I. A hunter
would stop and take us away with him. A day. A day would
come. Every day I sat by the side of the road. Watching them go
by. A day would come. He'd be young. Joseph's age. A hunter.

[*Loud music without any words. Then it softens*]

I can see it all: the hunter stops in front of the bungalow. A burst tyre. And Joseph helps him to change it. I can see her, too, the woman with the hunter: she's a platinum blonde, she smokes Player's 555, she is very made-up, very white. She is for Joseph. I take her and give her to Joseph. How I loved him, my quiet, wild little brother.

When he was fourteen, he went hunting panthers by the estuary, in broad sunlight. I remember, the mother saying he would be the death of her. He came back at night, with the dead panther in the prow of his boat. I started crying. He said the next time he'd take me with him.

[*Music*]

Together we'll leave the mother. Together we'll leave her behind. On the plain, alone with her madness.

[*Music*]

Without warning, while she's having her afternoon nap. She wakes up. She calls us. There's no one left to answer, no children left in the plain. She cooks the meal. There's no one left to eat it. The plain is empty. The mother will be punished. For having loved us.

[*Silence. Then music. Then the music gradually fades. They all stand still, their backs to the audience, waiting outside the unlit Bar (which is, of course, the same rectangular area as the bungalow). Then they go in. SUZANNE's voice goes on in the dark*]

That evening, there was a big black car in the yard outside the Bar in Réam. Inside it, waiting, sat a uniformed chauffeur.

[*Music*]

[*The bar lights up*]

[*Electric lighting: naked bulbs, a reddish, gloomy light. When the bar is fully lit the characters are already seated, motionless, frozen in the loud music and light. A powerful image. In the centre of the acting area is Mr JO. Dressed in white with a diamond ring on his finger and very strongly lit. The others are in shadow, looking at him. Except for SUZANNE. MR. JO looks at her*]

Mr. Jo was rich.

Mr. Jo's father had bought up the Red Lands plantations in North Cambodia during the rubber crisis, ten years before. Now he was re-selling them at exorbitant prices to foreign companies. The sole heir of this immense fortune was there that evening in Réam.

[*Music*]

The diamond on his left hand was enormous.

[*Pause*]

His suit was made of Chinese silk - tailored in Paris. The car was magnificent. He was alone. A millionaire. And he was looking at me.

[*Pause. Music. Scene without words: The MOTHER catches Mr JO looking at her daughter. She starts looking at her too. And the daughter is smiling at the heir to the Northern Plantations. Silently, the CORPORAL comes in and crouches on the floor. The MOTHER and the CORPORAL look at SUZANNE smiling at the son of the owner of the plantations. Not JOSEPH. JOSEPH looks down at the floor*]

[*Champagne is served at the tables*]

[*Loud music, then it fades*]

I knew the mother was frightened of dying while we were still so young. I understood my mother's glance. I smiled at the planter from the North.

[*Pause*]

It was my first prostitution.

[*Silence. Music, but soft. (The music must never interfere with the spoken words)*]

[*Mr JO rises and bows to the MOTHER*]

[*The MOTHER makes as if to get up*]

The Mother: [*Very softly*] But, of course... Please do...

[*Mr JO goes over and asks SUZANNE to dance*]

[*They dance*]

[*The MOTHER watches. Not JOSEPH. Perhaps JOSEPH is looking out at the harbour to avoid looking at SUZANNE. A slow conversation starts up between Mr JO and SUZANNE.*]

Mr. Jo: [*In a soft, distinguished voice*] Do you live round here?

Suzanne: Yes.

[*Pause*]

Is that your car in the yard?

Mr. Jo: Yes.

[*Pause*]

Would you do me the honour of introducing me to your mother?

Suzanne: Yes.

[Pause]

What make is it?

Mr. Jo: A Morris Leon Bollée. *[Pause]* My favourite make. *[Pause]*
Are you keen on cars, then?

Suzanne: Yes. *[Pause]* What horse-power is it?

Mr. Jo: Twenty-four I think.

Suzanne: *[Pause]* How much does a car like that cost?

Mr. Jo: *[Hesitant]* About fifty-thousand piastres, I think.

[SUZANNE stops dancing for a few seconds and looks at Mr JO]

Suzanne: That's incredible.

Mr. Jo: *[Surprised]* It's because it's a special model.

[No reply from SUZANNE who becomes pensive]

[JOSEPH stops looking out at the harbour. He looks at his sister. They look at each other. The MOTHER sees them. She's as if dazzled by Mr JO and disturbed by the look between JOSEPH and SUZANNE]

Mr. Jo: I'm here to supervise the loading of a cargo of latex...

[No reply from SUZANNE]

A pretty girl like you must get bored here on this plain... You're so young.

[No answer from SUZANNE]

[Loud music. They dance without speaking for a while]

[Mr JO is a good dancer. SUZANNE is preoccupied]

[The dance ends. The music starts up again at once]

[Mr JO and SUZANNE go over to the MOTHER's table]

[The MOTHER rises to greet Mr JO]

[JOSEPH remains seated. Mr JO sits down. Then SUZANNE]

[So they are all seated. There's champagne on the table, in front of them. They talk. SUZANNE speaks first]

Suzanne: *[To JOSEPH in a rush]* He's got a Morris Leon Bollée.

Mr. Jo: I've got a sports car that I like better.

Suzanne: Twenty-four horse-power.

Joseph: How many litres to the hundred kilometers?

Suzanne: How many?

Mr. Jo: Seventeen. In traffic, twenty.

Joseph: Does it hold the road well?

Mr. Jo: Yes. It does eighty like a bird. In the other one I can do a hundred easily.

Suzanne: It's worth fifty-thousand piastres.

The Mother: [*Thinking she's misheard*] What?

Mr. Jo: [*In the same even tone*] What kind do you have?

[*They look at each other without answering*]

The Mother: [*Pause*] Our's a Citroën.

Mr. Jo: Yes, you get more mileage out of a Citroën. And with a road like that...

[*JOSEPH and SUZANNE burst out laughing*]

Joseph: A hundred kilometers for twenty-four litres: that's what ours does.

Mr. Jo: Really?

Joseph: Instead of twelve...But then the carburettor's full of holes.

[*The MOTHER catches the children's laughter*]

Suzanne: If that was all it'd be nothing...if it was only the carburettor...But there's the radiator too...

[*Another outburst of laughter*]

[*Mr JO smiles, disconcerted*]

Joseph: It's a record...Fifty litres to the hundred kilometers.

The Mother: [*Repeats*] Fifty litres to the hundred kilometers.

Joseph: [*Taking up SUZANNE's joke*] If that was all it wouldn't be so bad...If it was only the carburettor and the radiator...

[*They all wait. Then an uncontrollable outburst of laughter*]

But there are the tyres...guess what our tyres are filled with...

[*Climax of laughter*]

Banana leaves...We stuff them with banana leaves.

[*Mr JO waits for the laughter to subside*]

Mr. Jo: It's certainly original...It's a scream, as they say in Paris.

[*No one pays any attention to him. They go on*]

Joseph: When we start out on a trip, we tie the Corporal onto the mudguard with a watering-can...

[*The three of them start laughing again*]

Suzanne: And put a hunting lamp on the front. Because as for our lights...Well, they haven't worked for ten years...

[*A pause in the laughter. Then they start up again*]

Joseph: And if it was only that... If it was only the car...But there were the sea-walls too...The sea-walls...

[*He can't talk any more he's laughing so much*]

[*Shrieks of laughter from the MOTHER and SUZANNE*]

The story of our sea-walls...It's enough to make you die laughing...

[*Laughter. More laughter. Mr JO is stupefied*]

We thought we could do it. Yes...We wanted [*Pause*] We wanted to hold back the Pacific.

Mr. Jo: And why would you want to hold back the Pacific? [*Pause as he remembers something*].Oh! yes...yes, I heard about it...The sea-walls. [*Pause*]. You were unlucky...A rotten piece of land...

Joseph: Yes...That's it...[*He points to the MOTHER*]. She didn't know.

The Mother: [*As if apologising*] I didn't know.

Suzanne: She didn't know anything. Not a thing.

Joseph: She wanted to hold back the Pacific...She thought she could.

Suzanne: She still thinks she can.

Joseph: It's true. Look at her. She still thinks it can be done.

[*They look at the MOTHER. The MOTHER looks somewhere else. Remains silent*]

Suzanne: [*Dreamily*] She must be a bit mad. [*Pause*]. We must all be a bit mad.

Joseph: [*Pointing to the mother*] She is. She's quite mad.

[*Suddenly the MOTHER looks frightened. JOSEPH goes on looking at her, then bursts out laughing again. SUZANNE does the same. And then the MOTHER too. The three of them are laughing at her, at her madness. The children repeat*]

Joseph and Suzanne: ...quite mad...quite mad...[*They go on saying this*]

[*The laughter stops. The music begins again, softly. The lights start to dim. Mr JO looks at SUZANNE. JOSEPH and SUZANNE are silent. Music. Mr JO offers JOSEPH a cigar. JOSEPH smokes it. The MOTHER is silent and half asleep*]

Mr. Jo: Can I see you again?

Suzanne: We live in the bungalow on the left of the Kampot road. At kilometre 184.

[*End of this scene*]

[*The lights grow very dim inside the bar*]

[*They all fall silent. SUZANNE's story continues*]

Suzanne's Voice: And so we got into the habit of letting Mr. Jo drive us into Réam. We liked riding in his car. [*Pause*]. It went on for a month. It cost us nothing. We drank champagne every night. We used to come home late. Our mother used to go to sleep in the Morris Léon Bollée on the way home.

It was my first affair. It was just as much Joseph's and my mother's affair really.

[*Pause*]

[*The light changes as SUZANNE speaks, the exterior becoming brightly lit, while the Bar-space grow dark. SUZANNE takes up her story again*]

He used to come in the afternoon, long before it was time to go to Réam.

[*Pause*]

We used to stay in the bungalow, he and I.

[*The bungalow lights up. Strong light matching sunlight outside*]

[*Mr JO and SUZANNE are sitting there alone*]

[*Again, the only difference between the bar and the bungalow resides in the lighting*]

[*The same wicker chairs, the same table, the same view (of the mountain)*]

[*Slowly the MOTHER and the CORPORAL cross the empty space behind the bungalow*]

[*The CORPORAL is carrying gardening tools. The mother wears a straw hat. They vanish*]

They're weeding round the banana trees. I don't know what Joseph is doing.

[*SUZANNE gets up and goes to the gramophone*]

[*Silence*]

[*She winds up the gramophone. Puts on a record*]

[*Music. The Eden Cinema Waltz*]

Mr. Jo had no choice. Either he never saw me alone, ever; or else he married me. The mother had said: marriage or nothing. She was full of hope. Sometimes I went to sleep. Then I'd wake up, and find Mr. Jo just where he'd been before, always under the mother's eye.

[*Pause*]

Joseph had said so too: marriage or nothing.

[*Music. The next scene is between the actors*]

Mr. Jo: That's a very old gramophone.

Suzanne: It's Joseph's. My mother bought it for him when she was at the Eden Cinema.

[*She turns towards the audience but without changing her position*]

You've already given me a blue dress, a compact, some nail varnish and lipstick, some expensive soap and beauty creams.

Mr. Jo: It's a very old model. I know something about gramophones. I've got an electric one at home. I brought it back from Paris.

Suzanne: Your electric gramophone's all right when there's electricity. There isn't any here.

Mr. Jo: There are battery operated just as good as electric ones.

Suzanne: Oh!

[*Silence and music*]

Mr. Jo: Suzanne...My little Suzanne...It's agony...Being so near to you and yet so far...

[*SUZANNE starts unfastening her dress*]

[*Music. SUZANNE stops undressing*]

[*SUZANNE goes on undressing*]

[*Mr JO gets up, comes over to her, then stops*]

[*In the distance, in the doorway, we see the MOTHER, who stops and looks*]

[*Mr JO goes outside. SUZANNE remains alone for a while*]

[*She looks suddenly exhausted, gloomy. She does up her dress. In the distance is the MOTHER, motionless*]

[*Mr JO comes back; he is followed by the CORPORAL carrying a huge parcel. They both go right round the bungalow, first on the roadside, then on the side where the audience is*]

[*Then JOSEPH arrives*]

[*JOSEPH and the MOTHER look at each other*]

[*The CORPORAL puts the package on the table*]

[*Everyone stands still and silent around the package*]

Suzanne's Voice: Nothing new had come to the plain for six years.

Mr. Jo: It's a gramophone. I'm like that. I keep my word. I hope you'll get to know me.

[*Mr JO goes over to the gramophone and starts to untie the strings*]

[*SUZANNE signs to him to stop*]

Suzanne: We must wait for them.

[*The Corporal has squatted down inside the room; he's waiting too*]

[*Mr JO looks outside, sees the MOTHER and JOSEPH standing, watching, and sits down. Then slowly SUZANNE turns towards the MOTHER and JOSEPH and gives them a long, loving smile*]

Suzanne's Voice: The gramophone was the price of Mr. Jo being allowed to look at me. I was giving it to Joseph, my brother, my little, since-dead, brother. How I loved him. Mr. Jo stood there crying.

Mr. Jo: I love you so much. I don't know what's happening to me. I've never felt like this before about anyone.

Suzanne: Don't say anything to *them.*

[*Pause*]

[*JOSEPH and the MOTHER enter the room*]

When they ask what it is, I'll tell them.

Mr. Jo: I mean nothing to you, less than nothing.

[*The MOTHER and JOSEPH walk around the package as if it wasn't there. The MOTHER sits down. JOSEPH goes out of the bungalow to have a shower. The CORPORAL waits outside the bungalow, now, facing the audience*]

[*The MOTHER talks about the CORPORAL to avoid talking about the package*]

The Mother: He's getting deafer and deafer.

Mr. Jo: I could never make out why you ever hired a deaf man. It's not as if labour was scarce around here.

[*The MOTHER doesn't answer*]

[*She sits down*]

[*Distant music. The package is still on the table*]

[*Enormous. Invisible*]

The Mother: [*To Mr JO*] You can stay to dinner if you'd like.

Mr. Jo: [*Startled*] Thank you very much, there's nothing I'd like better...

Suzanne: There's nothing to eat; always the same old wader-birds (Heron), they smell of fish and make you want to throw up. There's never anything else.

The Mother: It's very nourishing.

Mr. Jo: You don't know me, I have very simple tastes.

[*We hear the sound of running water*]

[*JOSEPH having a shower*]

[*The CORPORAL has been gone for some time. He comes back with a dish of steaming rice. Puts it on the table beside the dish of wader-bird*]

[*JOSEPH comes out of the shower. Into the room*]

[*Sees the dishes*]

[*Everyone is motionless around the package*]

[*At last SUZANNE speaks*]

Suzanne: It's a gramophone.

Joseph: We've got a gramophone already.

Mr. Jo: This is more up to date.

[*SUZANNE opens the package*]

[*The gramophone emerges. She shows it to Joseph, who winds it up. And, in front of Mr JO, questions SUZANNE*]

Joseph: Did you ask him for it?

Suzanne: No.

Joseph: Why did he give it to you?

Suzanne: [*Looking at Mr JO*] I don't know.

Suzanne: [*To Mr JO*] Why did you give it to me?

[*Mr JO starts to cry, and doesn't answer*]

[*JOSEPH puts on a record we already know: the Eden Cinema Waltz*]

[*The old theme emerges more clear, more perfect*]

[*Mr JO is still crying*]

[*And the miracle happens*]

[*JOSEPH and SUZANNE dance together*]

[*The mother watches them, enchanted*]

[*The CORPORAL watches them too*]

[*The dance becomes like something inherited by them both: they dance together like one body*]

[*Night falls*]

Suzanne's Voice: For us it was the most beautiful thing we'd ever heard. That music. The Eden Cinema Waltz.Everything became clear:When we went away, we'd be singing that tune.

[*They dance*]

The Mother: [*To Mr JO*] At least I've got two beautiful children. Look at them. They're very alike I think.

[*They go on dancing*]

Suzanne's Voice: That tune was the song of her death. Born of our longing for fabulous cities. Born of our impatience. Of our ingratitude. Of my love for my brother. The mother watched us. She was suddenly old. We were dancing on her dead body.

[*Music. And the dance goes on*]

The Mother: [*To Mr JO*] If I were you, I'd marry her. Look at her.

Mr. Jo: She's so young...It's terrible. My feelings for her are so strong.

The Mother: [*Gently*] I believe you. I believe it.

[*Pause*]

I suppose it's your father who's against it?

Mr. Jo: [*Prevaricating*] It takes more than a fortnight to decide about getting married.

The Mother: [*Still gentle*] Yes. In certain cases.

[*Pause*]

I'm going to die, you see. So I need to have my mind at rest about what's going to become of my little girl.

[*The bungalow slowly darkens, while the stage outside – the area representing the road, etc. – grows lighter*]

[*The characters leave the stage in the darkness*]

[*The scene changes with the music and the light*]

[*Distant shouts*]

[*We discover Mr JO and SUZANNE sitting outside the bungalow*]

[*She is wearing a blue dress*]

[*She is inexpertly made-up. She is doing her nails*]

[*Mr JO is watching. The MOTHER is inside the bungalow*]

[*She paces to and fro and looks – towards the audience – at SUZANNE and Mr JO*]

[*Then she goes towards the transparency at the back, where the road is supposed to be*]

[*There the CORPORAL is laying plants in the ground*]

Suzanne: You've damaged the bridge. You should leave the car on the road.

[*Stricken silence from Mr JO*]

She won't let us stay in the bungalow any more. We have to stay outside.

[*Music*]

What kind of car shall I have when we're married?

Mr. Jo: If we did get married. I think I'd be terribly unhappy. I can't think what to do to make you love me.

Suzanne: [*Taking up where she left off*] What kind of car?

Mr. Jo: A white Lancia. I've already told you...

Suzanne: And Joseph?

Mr. Jo: I don't know that I'll give Joseph a car... I can't promise.

[*SUZANNE is silent. Mr JO's frightened*]

[*Music throughout*]

It depends on you, as you well know. On how you treat me.

Suzanne: [*Gently*] You could give my mother a car, it would be the same thing: he could drive it.

Mr. Jo: [*In despair*] But there's never been any question of giving your mother a car. I'm not as rich as you seem to think.

Suzanne: [*Very calm*] If Joseph doesn't get a car, you can keep all your Lancia and marry whoever you please.

[*Mr JO turns to SUZANNE*]

Mr. Jo: [*Imploring*] You know quite well Joseph will get his car. You're turning me into someone horrible.

[*Mr JO takes SUZANNE's hand in his and kisses it*]

[*JOSEPH has appeared behind the transparency. He's helping the CORPORAL mend the bridge*]

[*The MOTHER joins them*]

[*SUZANNE looks down at the ground*]

Suzanne's Voice: The day before he had promised me a diamond ring if I'd go with him on a trip to the city. He told me that the diamond was at his place and that he was waiting for me to make up my mind before he brought it.

[*SUZANNE leans her head on her arm while we hear her voice*]

I asked how much it was worth: he didn't say exactly, but he did say it was worth more than the cost of the bungalow.

[*Music. Silence*]

I tried to work out how to get the diamond, how to get it out here on the plain, how to get it to my mother.

[*Music or silence*]

[*Mr JO looks at SUZANNE*]

[*The MOTHER watches both of them*]

Mr. Jo: You're so lovely. [*Pause*] And so desirable.

Suzanne: I'll be lovelier when I'm older.

Mr. Jo: When I've taken you away from here you'll leave me: I'm sure of it.

[*Mr JO looks crushed beneath the weight of his desire*]

Suzanne's Voice: He'd said he was staying on out here to supervise, overseeing the loading of the latex at Réam. But I knew he was to get the better of his father.

[*Music*]

He'd said: "Three days. Three days in the city. I won't touch you. We'll go to the cinema".

[*Music*]

[*JOSEPH roams round the couple. Crosses the front of the stage, goes out in the direction of the MOTHER. The MOTHER comes back towards the house, enters it and sits down*]

[*She wipes her forehead*]

[*JOSEPH and SUZANNE observe her*]

We were always afraid she'd die. Always. Every minute. One diamond worth the whole bungalow.

[*SUZANNE leaves Mr JO, goes into the bungalow and towards the MOTHER. She lifts her mother's feet onto a stool. Then goes out and comes back with a glass of water and some pills. The MOTHER is*] *passive. Takes the pills. Drinks the water. Distant sound of running water: JOSEPH having a shower. Mr JO moves forward and, with the audience, looks at the MOTHER and SUZANNE and their silent, fierce relationship. SUZANNE goes out again, comes back with a damp cloth which she puts on the MOTHER's forehead. Then she crouches beside the chair and starts fanning the MOTHER. The MOTHER starts to drowse, lulled by the regular movement. Quieter now, the MOTHER looks like a child. SUZANNE doesn't flinch. They speak to each other plainly, roughly]*

The Mother: Have you spoken to him about it?

Suzanne: I speak to him about it all the time.

[Pause]

It's his father. He wants his son to marry someone rich.

The Mother: Oh!

Suzanne: I don't think he's even mentioned me to his father yet.

[Pause]

But he'd gladly just go off with me.

The Mother: What do you mean?

[Then she understands without being told]

No.

[Pause. She pulls herself together]

And what do you want?

Suzanne: *[Pause]* Me? I want to stay with Joseph.

[The MOTHER considers, muttering to herself]

The Mother: Joseph...Always Joseph.

[Pause]

How old are you now? I forget.

Suzanne: Sixteen.

The Mother: *[Groans]* Sixteen...My god...My god.

[Silence]

[JOSEPH comes in. It looks as if he's been listening]

[Silence. Then the MOTHER speakes]

He's not going to marry her.

Joseph: Then, he'd better not come back any more.

[Silence or music]

[*Joseph goes out*]

Suzanne's Voice: I didn't mention the diamond. I was afraid of what she'd say. Just to hear what it was worth would have been enough to kill her.

[*Silence*]

[*The MOTHER falls asleep*]

[*SUZANNE goes back to the strip of land in front of the bungalow. Which lights up. With a white light. It's still early. The sun hasn't reached the mountain. SUZANNE sits down by M JO and looks around her. In the distance, inside the bungalow, the MOTHER is sleeping: the sleeping MOTHER is at the centre of everything*]

So it's all finished with Mr. Jo. I've already forgotten him. Children are still singing, riding on the buffaloes by the river. I can see them. Hear them. Hear their shrill little voices. There's no wind: the air's scorching hot.

[*Sound of children singing in the distance, in Cambodian*]

They were everywhere. Perched up in trees. Squatting by the creeks in the estuary. Alive. Dead. And as well as the children there were the stray dogs and the madmen of the plain. The children used to play with them.

[*SUZANNE looks at Mr JO who is sweltering in the heat*]

Suzanne: She doesn't want me to see you any more. It's all over.

[*Sounds of children. Evening noises*]

Mr. Jo: I can't accept that. I can't.

[*Silence*]

[*SUZANNE sings the song we heard on the gramophone*]

Mr. Jo: I love you, Suzanne.

Suzanne: She doesn't want to wait.

[*Pause*]

She knows your father's against me.

[*She starts to sing again*]

Mr. Jo: She's terrible.

[*Pause*]

Terrible, your mother.

Suzanne: Yes.

[*Pause*]

She's mad.

[*Pause*]

If we'd got married she'd have asked you for money to rebuild the sea-walls. So you see... She imagines them twice as big as before and built of concrete. So you see...

[*Pause*]

She'd have asked you to pay for having Joseph's teeth seen to. His teeth are in a very bad state. So you see...

[*SUZANNE laughs*]

Mr. Jo: I can't.. I can't accept it...

Suzanne: What?

Mr. Jo: Losing you...

[*SUZANNE laughs*]

Suzanne: So when do we get married?

Mr. Jo: [*Prevaricating*] I've told you: when you prove that you love me.

Suzanne: [*Laughing*] You mean when I've agreed to go on that trip. Three days with you, in Saigon.

[*She laughs. Mr JO doesn't answer*]

Suzanne: It's not true.

[*Pause*]

If we got married your father would disinherit you.

[*SUZANNE sings the gramophone tune*]

[*JOSEPH goes by. She half gets up and watches him disappear*]

Suzanne: I'm going for a swim with Joseph. We won't be coming to Réam with you any more.

[*Pause*]

Joseph agrees with her.

[*She gets up and goes*]

Mr. Jo: [*Without moving*] I've brought them.

[*SUZANNE halts*]

[*Stands there, her back still turned*]

Suzanne: What?

Mr. Jo: The diamonds.

[*Pause*]

You could just see which one you like best.

[*Pause*]

You never know.

[*She turns round slowly. He takes out a little tissue-paper package from his pocket: unfolds it. Three smaller packages fall out. SUZANNE comes over and looks at the rings held out in an open hand adorned with its own enormous diamond*]

Mr. Jo: They belonged to my mother. She was crazy about them....

[*SUZANNE looks at the rings and points to one of them*]

Suzanne: How much is that one worth ?

Mr. Jo: About twenty-thousand piastres: I don't know exactly.

[*Silence. Then music*]

[*In the distance the MOTHER wakes*]

[*She stands up and disappears inside the bungalow*]

Suzanne's Voice: I was familiar with figures. How much my mother owed, the price of an evening's work at the Eden Cinema, the price of a piano lesson or a French lesson, what I didn't know yet was the price of money. Suddenly, I felt immensely tired, exhausted, I remember: the plain suddenly looked strange. Everything had gone dark.

[*SUZANNE sits down, then lies down and looks at the diamond on her finger, closes her eyes*]

[*Silence. Music*]

[*Mr JO leans towards SUZANNE*]

Mr. Jo: My little Suzanne.... My treasure.

[*SUZANNE opens her eyes and looks at him*]

Mr. Jo: Is that the one you like best ?

Suzanne: It's the one that's worth most.

Mr. Jo: That's all you think about.

Suzanne: Yes.

Mr. Jo: You'll never love me...

[*Pause*]

Suzanne: Even if I did love you, we'd sell it.

Mr. Jo: It's hopeless.

[*Music*]

[*JOSEPH goes by in the distance*]

Suzanne's Voice: Joseph went by, on his way to the river. I called out to him. He stopped. He didn't see the diamond in my hand.

[*We see what is being described enacted. We don't hear the call. JOSEPH comes over to SUZANNE. Silently, she holds out her hand, shows him the diamond. JOSEPH shows no surprise. SUZANNE waits, still holding out her hand. Waits. No reaction from JOSEPH. Then she speaks*]

Suzanne: It's a diamond.

Joseph: What?

Suzanne: It's worth twenty thousand piastres.

[*JOSEPH smiles, as if at a childish joke*]

Joseph: Twenty thousand piastres.

[*He stops smiling and looks at Mr JO*]

[*A long pause*]

[*Mr JO lowers his eyes*]

Suzanne: He'll give it to me if I go with him.

Joseph: Where to?

Suzanne: The city.

[*JOSEPH looks at SUZANNE*]

Joseph: For ever ?

Suzanne: For three days.

Mr. Jo: [*Cries out*] Suzanne hasn't understood.... She hasn't understood.... It's my only chance.

[*JOSEPH is silent. Then looks at the bungalow, as if making a calculation. He looks at Mr JO. He looks at SUZANNE, and is silent. Then, suddenly, far off, the MOTHER's voice, shouting. At first, we can't understand what she's saying. Then she comes into the visible part of the bungalow followed by the CORPORAL. It's the CORPORAL she was and still is talking to: to the CORPORAL, who can't hear a word. That's why she's shouting. She sits down at a table and starts to write, building her sea-walls all over again. The CORPORAL sits at her feet, listening to words he can't hear. But what the MOTHER says is quite precise, even if barely audible, even to the audience*]

The Mother: What we should do is dig deeper.... get down past the mud.... and on to the clay....[*Pause*]. Reinforce the banks all along the river and on the other side of the bungalow... but above all get the props down deep, at least a metre deep... try to reach the clay, get past the mud... it all depends on that... and every so often, lay down concrete foundations... You can buy half price cement at Réam. That's not the problem... the problem is to dig through the mud and reach... reach the bottom of the marsh, the clay... that's what was missing the first time... concrete... remember the millions of crabs that got through the sea-walls... then the tide came through...[*Pause*]. We mustn't delude ourselves about the first year, there'll still be some salt left... We'll have to wait till all the soil's been washed right through, right down to the clay... It'll take at least three years if you ask me... etc, etc.

[*This all goes on at the same time as the scene between JOSEPH, SUZANNE and Mr JO. None of these three pays any attention to the MOTHER and the CORPORAL. JOSEPH goes off without a word. SUZANNE takes the ring off her finger and holds it out to Mr JO who takes it, and puts it in his pocket. Then stands there, crushed*]

Mr. Jo: Now you've wrecked everything.

Suzanne: I don't want to go with you. I still feel the same about it.

[*Mr JO cries*]

I'd have told him sooner or later about the diamond. I couldn't have helped it.

[*Silence. Still, in the background, we can hear the loud confused mutterings of the MOTHER about the new sea-walls. JOSEPH goes by, not looking at SUZANNE*]

I don't think you should bother to come back.

Mr. Jo: It's terrible... terrible... Why would you have to tell him?

Suzanne: You shouldn't have shown it to me. You can't understand.

[*Mr JO cries. She is silent*]

Mr. Jo: It's terrible... I can't Suzanne, I can't give you up... I can't.

[*Silence*]

Suzanne's Voice: I wanted to go into the forest with Joseph. It was the best moment, in the cool of the evening freshness, to go to the villages on the mountain. Mr. Jo looked as if he was suffering torments.

[*Silence*]

I called Joseph. I told him it would be a good idea to go to the mountain tonight. He came. I stood up. It was then, I think, that

Mr. Jo cried out. He said he'd give me the diamond anyway.

[*JOSEPH and SUZANNE freeze. The MOTHER suddenly stops talking*]

[*Silence. No further sound. Then Mr JO goes over to SUZANNE*]

[*He gives SUZANNE the ring*]

[*Everyone watches: the MOTHER, JOSEPH, the CORPORAL*]

[*And suddenly SUZANNE runs towards the bungalow. Reaches it*]

[*She holds out the ring to the MOTHER*]

[*The MOTHER holds out her hand. The bungalow goes dark*]

[*The rest of this scene takes place in the darkened bungalow*]

[*Lights only outside. We don't see SUZANNE speaking*]

> She took the ring and looked at it. Then she asked me how much
> it was worth. I said twenty thousand piastres and that he'd given
> it to me. She seemed not to take it in. I repeated what I'd said.
> That it was worth twenty thousand piastres and he'd given it to
> me. Suddenly I could scarcely recognise her. She went into her
> room and shut the door. I knew she'd gone to hide the ring. She
> always hid everything: quinine, tinned food, tobacco. In crevices
> in the wall, in her mattress. She hid things on herself too, tied
> round her body under her clothes.

[*Music*]

[*The bungalow lights up. And now it's night outside. There are three,
the three of them, in a different time sequence from the narration:
SUZANNE and JOSEPH are eating. Not the MOTHER. Silence. Then,
again, SUZANNE describes what happened – which we have not seen*]

> Then she came back from hiding the ring, she threw herself on
> me and beat me. She was shouting. Joseph came in. At first he let
> her beat me, and then he took her in his arms and kissed her.

[*Music*]

> She wept. We all wept. Together. All three of us.

[*Music*]

> And then we all laughed.

[*The following scene is between the actors. Direct dialogue, but
disjointed, as the telling of the story has been: it's the scene which must
have followed the beating, the tears, the laughter*]

The Mother: What did you say to him?

Suzanne: I explained it all. A ring is nothing to him.

Joseph: You mustn't worry about her any more. It's all over.

Suzanne: You mustn't worry about Joseph any more, either.

The Mother: I probably worry too much. You're right.

[*Pause*]

Just look at the way she handled Mr. Jo! But you're right. I can't stop worrying: ever.

[*She shouts*]

But it's not just the rich who have things: if we want it, we can be rich too.

[*The children repeat the MOTHER's last sentence*]

Suzanne: The mother fell asleep while we were having dinner. As he was putting her to bed, Joseph saw Mr. Jo's ring in a string round her neck.

[*Music*]

[*Dinner. The mother falls asleep*]

[*The light fades again*]

While she was sleeping, we went to the village on the mountain to buy some chickens. To eat on the way, Joseph said. Because the next morning we were leaving for Saigon, to sell Mr Jo's diamond.

END OF THE FIRST PART

Part Two

*In the front of the stage, in a yellow light, the MOTHER sits on a red
sofa - in extremely bad taste - with brightly coloured pink and green
cushions and two fair-ground dolls. She wears a straw hat, black shoes,
much-mended cotton stockings and her dark red dress. She's holding a
big, bulging handbag. SUZANNE sits next to her, "made-up like a tart",
in a blue dress, also with a straw hat and a handbag. They are sitting
side by side as if on a train.*

*On a small table behind them is a notice: "For Sale. Magnificent
Diamond". Once more there is a silence before anyone speaks, while
the background noises are established: city noises - shouts of market
traders, bicycles, squeaking of streetcars, car horns, the click-clack of
mah-jong games, clogs on cobbles, etc.*

Suzanne: The Central Hotel looked out on the Mekong River on one
side, and on the other, on the tramway between Cholen and
Saigon. The hotel was run by Carmen, Mademoiselle Marthe's
daughter. Mademoiselle Marthe had worked in a brothel in Saigon
harbour. She'd bought the hotel for her daughter.

Both Mademoiselle Marthe and Carmen were very fond of the
mother. For years they'd let her stay in the hotel for nothing.
Now, again, Carmen had tried to help her. She'd tried to sell the
diamond to the guests staying in the hotel. But none of them
would buy it. So, the mother decided to sell the diamond herself.

The first dealer she takes it to offers her ten thousand piastres.

He says it's got a serious flaw, what's known in the trade as a
"toad". It halves it's value. The mother doesn't believe it. She
wants twenty thousand piastres. She goes to another dealer. Then
to a third, then to a fourth. They all point out the toad. The
mother persists. She still wants twenty thousand piastres. The less
they offer the more she wants her twenty thousand. Twenty
thousand piastres is what the new sea-wall will cost, the one she
wants to build before she dies. She's offered eleven thousand
piastres. Six thousand. Eight thousand. She refuses. This goes on

for a week. She goes out every morning. She comes back every evening when it gets dark. First she goes to the white dealers. Then to the others. The Indians. And finally to the Chinese in Cholen. For a week Joseph and I wait for her to come out of the dealers' shops. Then, one evening, Joseph doesn't come back to the hotel. He's gone off in the Citroën. The mother doesn't pay much attention to Joseph's disappearance. She's obsessed with the diamond. She's already beginning to identify Mr. Jo with the "toad" in the heart of the diamond.

[*Silence*]

[*SUZANNE smiles at the MOTHER. The MOTHER looks at her. This interruption of their stillness must be performed in silence. It's as if the MOTHER were trying to remember something*]

The Mother: "I ought to have been suspicious of that toad right from the beginning. Right from the moment I met him in the bar at Réam."

[*The MOTHER smiles*]

Suzanne's Voice: And then, one evening, she gets it into her head that she must find Mr. Jo.

[*Music*]

She tells me *she'll* find Mr. Jo in the city, and then she'll bring him to me. I promise the mother to ask him for the two other diamonds he showed me out on the plain. The mother waits for Mr. Jo outside cinemas. Looks for him in cafés, outside luxury shops, in hotel lobbies. She never finds him.

[*Pause*]

[*SUZANNE gets up and moves away from the MOTHER*]

[*The MOTHER remains alone*]

[*SUZANNE looks at her. The MOTHER doesn't move*]

[*It should be a terrible moment*]

Suzanne: So what did she do, my mother? She tried to sell me instead of the diamond. Yes, my mother wanted to sell me instead of the diamond. She asked Carmen to find a man who would take me far away, for ever. The mother want to be alone.

[*The MOTHER slowly turns and looks at SUZANNE. A shattering look, denying nothing, excusing nothing*]

[*Pause*]

She doesn't want children any more.

[*Music. SUZANNE buries her face in her hands*]

[*The MOTHER turns away. They are cut off from one another*]

> Carmen makes me sleep in her room. She doesn't want me to sleep with my mother any longer. She is frightened for me.

[*Music*]

> Carmen tells me I must forget the mother: says we should free ourselves of our love for her. That any kind of marriage would be better: "Any man'll do," she says. "You can take up with somebody else after a couple of months". But I must leave my mother. She's crazy.

[*Music*]

[*SUZANNE changes her position; goes and stands behind the MOTHER*]

[*All of SUZANNE'S movements should produce a sense of great violence*]

> She's a monster of destruction. The things she can make people believe! The things she made the peasants on the plain believe!

> She ruined their peace. And now she wants to start all over again. Sell her children and start again. She wants to overcome the force of the winds, the force of the tides. To be stronger than the Pacific. She still imagines roads over the waters of the Pacific. And fields of rice.

[*SUZANNE moves away from the MOTHER*]

[*The MOTHER senses this movement; she looks as if she's sorry for having been so outrageous*]

[*Music*]

[*SUZANNE moves again. Turns away from the MOTHER*]

[*The MOTHER lowers her eyes*]

Suzanne's Voice: Carmen does my hair. Dresses me up. Gives me some money. She tells me to go into the city. And forget. I take Carmen's clothes, and her money. I go to the fashionable part of the town.

[*SUZANNE stands motionless, facing the audience*]

> It is five o'clock in the afternoon. The whites are feeling refreshed after the siesta. They've taken their evening shower. They're dressed in white. White linen. They're off to the tennis courts. I'm looking for Joseph, my little brother.

[*She walks to the music of the waltz, while the MOTHER watches with the elemental smile that means "my child"*]

> The sun has already set. The sprinklers are going along the Boulevard Catinat. It's hot: soon the monsoon will descend on Indochina. I'm lost. My dress pains me, my whore's dress. My face

pains me too. And my heart. I'm ugly. The whole city knows it. It's laughing at me. I'm pursued by laughter. By stares. I have no mother any more. No brother. I'm going to die of shame. That old bitch, my mother, where is she now? Chasing around somewhere in the city. Without me.

[*Pause*]

It'll be Joseph who kills her. He's started already. My brother: where is he? Lost somewhere in the city. The liar.Lost amid all the vulgarity, among all these ordinary people. I'm looking for him, to kill him.

[*Music. Loud at first, then softer*]

I go back to the Eden Cinema. The piano's still there. The lid's shut. I weep.

[*Music. Softer still. SUZANNE looks at the MOTHER. The MOTHER looks at her. SUZANNE goes over to her, sits down beside her*]

Tonight, I want to sleep with her, my mother, in her room. She's started to wait for Joseph. She's losing hope about selling the diamond. All hope. She speaks.

[*SUZANNE leans towards the MOTHER. Embraces her*]

[*Silence*]

The Mother: [*Quietly*] Carmen's found someone.

[*Pause*]

He's called Barner. He travels for a factory in Calcutta.

[*Pause*]

It's a good job.

[*Pause*]

He'd give thirty thousand piastres.

[*Pause*]

You'd go away for ever.

[*SUZANNE doesn't answer*]

[*The MOTHER goes on absently*]

Perhaps Joseph's dead. Why shouldn't he be...? He could have been run over by a tram...

Suzanne: [*Quietly*] No.

The Mother: [*Indifferent*] Oh. [*Pause*] You think he'll come back?

Suzanne: Yes.

[*Silence. Music*]

The Mother: He's called Barner. He's English.

[*Pause*]

He's forty.

[*Pause*]

His mother's still alive.

[*Pause*]

He works for a big cotton manufacturer in Manchester. In England. He wants to get married. He's been talking about it for years.

[*Pause*]

Carmen offered him the diamond. He almost bought it. [*Pause*] He'd have liked to buy it for his mother.

[*Pause*]

And then he couldn't make up his mind. But he'd buy it for his wife.

[*Pause*]

Which would make... thirty thousand piastres plus twenty thousand piastres: fifty thousand piastres.

[*Silence. SUZANNE doesn't move*]

[*The MOTHER has been speaking mechanically, without energy, without conviction*]

The Mother: [*Lifeless*] You know, if Joseph doesn't come back, it would be safer.

[*Silence*]

[*Then the MOTHER starts stroking her child's hair, very gently, as if thinking of something else. SUZANNE huddles to her mother's body*]

Well?

Suzanne: I'd prefer a hunter.

The Mother: [*With a distant smile*] Why a hunter? Why is it always a hunter?

[*Silence*]

[*No answer from SUZANNE*]

[*The MOTHER goes on talking, without waiting for SUZANNE to reply*]

The Mother: A hunter. You can always find a hunter.

[*Pause*]

Well.... Yes....

[*Pause*]

I'll tell him you don't want to leave me. That's what I'll tell him.

Suzanne: Yes.

[*Silence*]

[*SUZANNE lifts her head and looks at the MOTHER. SUZANNE speaks roughly. The MOTHER is distant, dim, listless. Does she believe SUZANNE's lies? Impossible to guess*]

Suzanne: Joseph will come back.

The Mother: Oh.

Suzanne: I saw him. In the Boulevard Catinat. He told me he'd be back.

[*Pause*]

He met a woman at the cinema.

The Mother: Oh... So he'll be going away.

Suzanne: [*Pause*] No... He'll come back. I saw Mr. Jo, too.

The Mother: Oh.

Suzanne: I spoke to him about the diamonds.

[*Pause*]

The Mother: Oh... He wouldn't discuss it?

Suzanne: No.

The Mother: And what about marrying you ?

Suzanne: Nothing. Still the same.

The Mother: [*Pause*] Is it his father?

Suzanne: [*Pause*] I think so. [*Pause*] They don't want to have anything to do with us.

[*Pause*]

The Mother: Oh well... I see their point...

Suzanne: [*Pause*] Yes.

[*Music*]

[*They're silent*]

[*The MOTHER seems to be thinking. Closes her eyes*]

[*Half-closes them*]

The Mother: [*Reflectively*] I've already forgotten what Mr. Jo looks like.

[*Pause*]

Suzanne: Don't think about him.

[*Music*]

The Mother: What have you been doing ?

Suzanne: I went to the Eden Cinema.

[*Pause*]

The piano's still there.

[*Pause*]

Not used any more.

[*The MOTHER wanders off into her memories of the Eden Cinema*]

The Mother: [*Pause*] There was a time when I thought of buying it.

[*Pause*]

I didn't say anything about it.

[*Pause*]

So that you could go on with your music...

[*Pause*]

You were quite good at it. Weren't you?

Suzanne: I don't know.

The Mother: But you see....

[*Silence*]

[*The MOTHER sits rigid, upright*]

[*The light dims. SUZANNE puts her arms around her MOTHER*]

[*The MOTHER just sits there*]

[*Blackout*]

Suzanne's Voice: That evening, I slept clinging to her body. To my mother's body. It was as if she'd already forgotten me. But her smell was there. The smell of the plain.

[*Music. A child's sobs - SUZANNE's sobs - in the darkness*]

Then, the next morning, Joseph came back.

[*Loud music. Long silence*]

[*Then light on part of the stage*]

[*SUZANNE and the MOTHER straighten up as if they've just heard a noise. They wait. Facing the audience. JOSEPH appears in the light. He*]

*doesn't look at them, doesn't look at anything. They don't turn round.
JOSEPH goes up to them. They wait. Everyone motionless. Then:*]

He said he'd come to fetch us. To go back to the plain.

[*JOSEPH turns away. SUZANNE looks at JOSEPH*]

He's got thinner. He's smoking American cigarettes. He looks as if
he hasn't slept for several nights. Sometimes, at Prey-Nop, when
he came home from hunting, he used to look like that. Through
his anger at having to take us back, I can see that Joseph is
marvellously happy. And that he's finished with us and with the
plain. He goes up to (our) mother and says he's sold the diamond
for the price she wanted: twenty thousand piastres. His voice is
gentle, almost unrecognisable.

[*JOSEPH silently puts the twenty thousand piastres on the table, not
looking at the MOTHER. The MOTHER keeps her back turned, doesn't
look around. She seems to be listening*]

[*It's SUZANNE who picks up the money and gives it to the MOTHER. The
MOTHER takes the money, looks at it, and puts it in her handbag*]

[*Everyone is motionless as SUZANNE looks at her brother*]

I think: if I die, he'll look at me. I don't die.

[*JOSEPH looks at SUZANNE. They look at each other*]

[*The MOTHER is isolated*]

[*They stop looking at each other. At anything. They wait. Standing up,
motionless. As if all three of them were lost*]

[*That part of the stage gradually darkens, and at the same time, the
bungalow-space lights up very slowly and we find ourselves back there
again. While this lighting change is taking place, they all go off in the
direction opposite to the one JOSEPH came in by*]

[*Music*]

Our mother talked the whole way back. About the new sea-walls
she had to build before she died. About a new method of
building them. By digging down to the bottom of the marsh. The
trouble was the salt. She'd invented the new method lying awake
at night. By the time we reached the last white outpost before the
Réam road, it was six o'clock in the evening.

[*The light changes*]

Joseph got some gas. When he paid, he pulled a bunch of ten
piastre notes out of his pocket. The mother saw it. She didn't talk
any more. Joseph sat down on the running-board of the Citroën:

he ran his fingers through his hair like someone just waking up. He wasn't alone. He was with her, the woman he'd met at the Eden Cinema. From now on, wherever he went he'd be with her. We could already see the Elephant mountains, its trees, gradually being swallowed up by the dark. Joseph looked at the forest. He wouldn't be going hunting there any more. He stretched himself, slowly, and at length. Then he said he was hungry. Those were the first words he'd spoken since we left Saigon.

The mother had some sandwiches that Carmen had made up for the journey. We ate them. While we were eating them she quietened down at last. I think she'd been frightened, our mother, of not even having to cook for us any more. Of not having even that much left.

Joseph: When she woke up, it must have been about two in the morning. The car was going along, quite smoothly. She got the blanket out from under the seat. She said she was cold.

Suzanne: It was then that Joseph suddenly remembered. [*Pause*]. He felt in his pockets and held something out to the mother. In the palm of his hand.

[*The CORPORAL enters. Rearranges furniture: brings in tea service*]

I saw it too. In the palm of his hand lay Mr. Jo's diamond. The mother gave a cry.

[*Music*]

Joseph said Carmen had given him the diamond to sell the day before. And he'd sold it. And then he'd been given it back. There was no point in trying to understand. The mother took the diamond. Reluctantly. She put it away in her handbag.

[*Pause*]

Then she started to cry again.

[*The CORPORAL has gone into the bungalow. He brings in steaming hot tea*]

We didn't ask her why she was crying. We knew. She'd hoped this time would have been the last. That after this trip to the city there'd be nothing more to do, no trying to sell again, no more money to be got. The thought of the twenty thousand piastres that could be got from selling the diamond again appalled her.

[*Music*]

[*The MOTHER goes into the bungalow*]

[*The CORPORAL brings her hot tea. They drink it: the CORPORAL and the MOTHER*]

> Far away, towards Siam, the sun was rising. Towards the Pacific it was still dark.

[*The light increases gradually*]

[*Deep silence*]

[*No music*]

> It was in the days that followed, just before Joseph left, that our mother wrote her last letter to the Land Commission in Kampot.

[*In the silence the MOTHER straightens up and starts to read out (or recite) the letter. The CORPORAL listens. The MOTHER, too, listens to her own letter. While she reads, neither JOSEPH nor SUZANNE is visible*]

The Mother: Prey-Nop. 24th March 1931.

> Gentlemen, I am writing to you once again to tell you this: No one will come here, after me. If you ever manage to evict me, and come to show the concession to some new tenant, a hundred peasants will crowd around and say to the new tenant: "Dip your finger into the mud of the rice fields and taste it. Do you think rice can grow in salt? You'll be the fifth tenant of this concession. The others are all dead or ruined".

> I know how powerful you are, and that by virtue of the power invested in you by the Government of the Colony, the whole plain is in your hands. I know too that all my knowledge of your wickedness, and the wickedness of your colleagues, of those who preceded you is useless if I alone possess it. This is something it took me a long time to learn. But now I know. And so there are already hundreds of others in the plain who know what you're like.

[*Pause*]

> This is a long letter. I can't sleep any more, since my misfortunes, since the sea-walls were swept away. I hesitated a long time before writing this letter to you. But now it seems to me that I was wrong not to have written it before.

> To make you take an interest in me, I have to talk to you about yourselves. Only about how wicked you are, perhaps - but anyway about yourselves. And if you read this letter, I am sure you will read all future letters, if only to find out how much I

have progressed in the knowledge of your wickedness. I've talked to all the people who came to build the sea-walls, and I never tire of telling them what you're like.

[*Pause*]

I've talked to my children too. I always told myself I'd tell them when they were older, so as not to spoil their childhood. Now they know.

A lot of children die here. The only workable land in the plain is full of the bodies of dead children. So I - so that at last their deaths may serve some purpose, you never know - I tell the people what you're like. It's a long time now since I first started turning these things over in my mind at night. It's been so long that all this misery has served no purpose that I'm beginning to hope a time will come when it will be of some use. And that when my children go away forever, young as they are, they'll know about the consequences of your wickedness: perhaps, that will be something to be going on with.

[*Pause*]

Where is the money I earned, the money I saved sou by sou to buy this concession? The money I brought you one morning, seven years ago? That morning, I gave you everything I possess, everything. It was as if I had offered up my own body as a sacrifice, so that out of my ashes a whole future of happiness for my children might spring. And you took that money. You took it quite matter-of-factly and I went away happy. It was the most glorious moment in my life. It still amazes me. I can see you now: you knew you'd just sold me land riddled with salt. You knew I was throwing everything I had into the Pacific. And you just smiled politely. How can men be like you and still look like ordinary people? How can people steal from the poor and grow rich on their hunger without their wickedness being visible? Without it killing you too?

You have been my obsession, for the last seven years. Soon I'll be left alone on this impossible land and this is what I'll do. I'll see that all the officials of the Land Commission in Kampot are killed. Every one. How better could I fill the emptiness of my life? And so I say to the peasants: when you kill them, don't any of you admit it. Or else all of you admit it. If a thousand of you are guilty, they can't do anything.

I repeat, for the last time, we must have something to live for.

And if it is not the hope, however vague, of new sea-walls, it will have to be the hope of corpses, even if they are only the loathsome corpses of the officials of the Kampot Land Commission.

[Music]

Suzanne's Voice: This letter never reached the officials of the Kampot Land Commission. It was found near the mother's body after her death, together with a final demand for the rent. Mr. Jo's diamond was still on a string around her neck.

[*The bungalow becomes completely lit*]

[*Silence. It is day. The MOTHER sleeps*]

[*As if her own story had rocked her to sleep*]

[*The CORPORAL lowers a blind to shade the MOTHER'S sleeping body*]

[*Her body is no longer visible: it has become a dark shadow in the white light*]

[*Silence*]

For a week after we got back Joseph stayed in bed. He only got up in the evening to eat. Then he'd sit on the veranda looking at the mountain, at the forest. We knew he'd soon be leaving. One afternoon, during the siesta, he called me. Said he wanted to tell me what had happened. So that I'd remember afterwards, when he was gone. And later on, too. And also because he was afraid he might forget it himself, later on, when he had forgotten this particular love affair. We went and sat by the river, in the shade of the bridge, away from her, our mother.

[*Music*]

[*The bungalow is lit round the outside, but the black shadow of the MOTHER's body is still visible*]

[*JOSEPH and SUZANNE come to the river separately*]

[*She sits or lies down some distance away from him*]

I listened to Joseph's story. But he was talking to himself. He didn't see me.

Joseph: It happened at the Eden Cinema. One evening. She arrived late. I didn't notice her at first. There was a man with her. I think I saw him first. Suddenly I heard very heavy breathing, right next to me. It was him. She saw me looking at him and turned towards me. She smiled. She said: "It's always like this". I said: "Always?" She said: "Yes, always." I asked her who he was. She laughed.

She said he was her husband. She took out a packet of cigarettes from her bag, Players 555. She asked for a light. I gave her one.

[*Pause*]

I saw her hands. Her eyes. She was looking at me. Her hand was very slim and supple. [*Pause*] It felt almost as if the bones were broken. We didn't talk any more. I don't know how long it went on. The lights were going up. I let go of her hand. But it sought mine again. I thought I'd leave. But I couldn't. I said to myself, she must be used to picking men like this in cinemas. The lights went up. Her hand was withdrawn. I didn't dare look at her. She, yes, she dared - she looked at me. The man had suddenly woken up. I thought he was rather good looking. She pointed me out to him. She said: "He's a hunter from Réam". We'd left the cinema. I was just behind her. They went up to an eight-cylinder Delage. The man turned round, said to me: "Are you coming?" I said: "Yes".

[*Music. The Eden Cinema Waltz*]

We stopped at a night-club. "We'll have a whisky" said the man. It was then I understood. When he had that whisky. We left that club. Went on to another one near the port. Had more to drink. And so it went on. And on. Suddenly, it was morning. I asked myself what I was doing there, with those people. It was six o'clock in the morning. The man had fallen asleep with his head on the table. She leaned towards me, stretching over him. We kissed. I felt as if I'd died. I'm rather hazy about what happened next. I remember there were gardens round the night-club, waterfalls, swimming pools. Everything was....very light....and empty... emptied... I drove the Delage. We went to a hotel. We stayed there for a week. Once she asked me to tell her about my life. I told her about the diamond. She told me to fetch it. Said she'd buy it. When I got back to the Central Hotel I found it in my pocket, together with the money.

[*JOSEPH has stopped talking*]

[*JOSEPH and SUZANNE remain as they are*]

[*They look at the bungalow*]

[*The CORPORAL pulls up the blind and the shadow over the MOTHER vanishes*]

[*Then the CORPORAL comes and goes with hot rice and hot tea. No one else moves*]

Suzanne's Voice: The mother was waiting for Joseph to leave. She
didn't want to cook for us any more. It was the Corporal who
bought the rice bread, who cooked wader-bird stew. The mother
didn't speak any more. She just sat in a chair, facing the Pacific.
With her back to the road. She never looked at us once during all
that time. She didn't try to sell the diamond again. One day she
asked me to sell Mr. Jo's gramophone. I put it in a bag and gave
it to the driver of the Réam bus to give to Agosti, a planter in
Réam. Another time I took Mr. Jo's presents, the blue dress, the
compact, the nail polish, and threw them in the river. That meant
there was nothing left to sell. I remember those days: like a long-
drawn-out deathbed. The sun. The drought. It gave everyone a
fever. The waiting lasted a month.

[*Music*]

Then one evening... It was eight o'clock...

[*Headlights appear suddenly, flooding the stage, the bungalow. They
are all three of them there: and the CORPORAL, too, sitting by the
MOTHER. All are transfixed by the light*]

No one heard the car coming, not even Joseph. She must have
been there some time, waiting on the other side of the bridge,
before she decided to sound her horn. Then she sounded the
horn.

[*Music*]

[*JOSEPH gets up and goes over to the MOTHER*]

[*The MOTHER, still turned towards the Pacific, lies back in her chair.
Careful, suddenly. She's very pale*]

[*It's almost as if she hadn't heard. For the first time since they got back
from the city, JOSEPH looks at the MOTHER*]

Joseph: I'll be back.

The Mother: Yes.

[*Music*]

Joseph: I'll be back in a few days.

The Mother: Yes.

[*Music*]

Joseph: [*Insists*] I'll come back. We'll sell up everything. I'll take you
both away.

The Mother: Yes.

[*Music*]

[*The MOTHER doesn't move*]

[*Suddenly, a huge light inside the bungalow*]

[*SUZANNE looks*]

Joseph: I'm leaving everything here. Even my guns.

[*Pause*]

[*The MOTHER doesn't answer*]

[*He turns towards SUZANNE*]

Tell her I'll be back.

Suzanne: He'll be back.

Joseph: A week from now.

Suzanne: [*Repeats*] He'll be back a week from now.

[*The MOTHER doesn't speak. She shuts her eyes*]

[*No one moves*]

[*JOSEPH crouches by the MOTHER and looks at her all over but doesn't touch her*]

[*Then he looks at SUZANNE*]

[*The headlights sweep over the forest, over the road, over the sleeping village, then over the MOTHER, SUZANNE and JOSEPH*]

[*The car has been turned round and is now facing towards the city*]

[*JOSEPH looks at the road. Looks again at the MOTHER, gets up, goes off*]

[*The headlights recede. Disappear*]

[*Music*]

[*The CORPORAL comes in with hot rice - just as he always does. But this time he stays. The MOTHER speaks*]

The Mother: Go and eat.

Suzanne: [*Crying out in rage*] No.

The Mother: Very well. He'll leave her. He'll leave everyone and everything.

Suzanne: [*Still shouting*] Be quiet!

The Mother: The longest he'll ever have stayed anywhere will be here on the plain.

[*Pause*]

I'll be quiet now.

[*Music*]

[*The CORPORAL helps the mother to undress. Takes her into the next room*]

[*SUZANNE remains for a moment crouched on the floor of the room, her face almost touching the ground*]

[*Then she goes out*]

[*The bungalow darkens*]

[*Music. The Eden Cinema waltz*]

[*Day breaks*]

[*Sunlight*]

[*SUZANNE comes towards the audience*]

[*Sits down. Talks to us*]

[*Music*]

Suzanne: Three weeks went by in which nothing happened. The mother slept. I spent all day by the road waiting for hunters. Every three hours I went in to look after my mother. She'd had an attack the day after Joseph left. The doctor came from Réam: heart trouble.

[*Music*]

Then one evening Agosti came. He'd heard there was a girl all on her own at Prey-Nop. So he came. I took him in to see my mother. He told her he had started a pineapple farm. They sold well, he used artificial fertilisers. In three years' time he'd be able to leave the plain. My mother said Agosti's land was healthy but in her concession anything like that was impossible, because of the salt. Then she fell silent.

[*Music*]

I went into the forest with Agosti. It was cool under the trees, after all those fields of pineapple. Cool and dark.

[*Long pause*]

He took out his handkerchief and wiped the blood from my dress and from me. Night fell there in the forest.

[*Distant music*]

That night, for the first time, I slept in Joseph's room. It was just as he'd left it. With his guns, some empty cartridges, a pack of cigarettes. The bed was unmade. If Joseph had been there I'd have told him what had happened with Agosti. But he wasn't here any more. I remember that night. The forest and the Pacific all round the house. The sound of the wind. Beating against the mountainside. Sweeping over where I lay.

[*Silence*]

Agosti came back the next day. He asked me if I'd marry him. I said no. Said I'd rather go away with Joseph when he came back.

[*Distant music*]

[*SUZANNE walks slowly across the stage*]

[*Then she stops and sits down facing the audience, while the bungalow darkens, goes quite dark*]

And then a letter came from Joseph. He said he was all right. That we could write to him at the Central Hotel.

[*Music. Death theme*]

And then the mother died. One afternoon. I was in the forest with Agosti. She'd told me to go out with him.The Corporal was there to look after her. When I came back she couldn't breathe. Gasps and groans issued from her body, and moans addressed to her children.

[*Silence*]

Agosti went back to Réam to phone the Central Hotel.

[*Music. Death theme*]

By evening my mother had stopped moaning. Her face grew strange. First it looked weary. Then extremely happy. And then she wanted to talk again: one last time.

[*SUZANNE hides her face in her hands*]

I told her I was there, I spoke my name, and said I was her child. She didn't seem to take it in. Didn't seem to remember. It can't have been to us, to her children, that she wanted to speak one last time, but to someone beyond us, to others. Who knows? To many, many others perhaps, to whole nations, to the world. Before she died a smile flickered over her lips and over her closed eyes. Then vanished. By the time Agosti got back, my mother's heart had stopped.

[*Music*]

[*The MOTHER is still there, sitting in the bungalow, while her death is being described*]

[*The CORPORAL helps her to lie down on the camp bed he has set out on the stage. So the MOTHER lends herself, while still alive, to the enactment of her dying*]

[*And now it's over*]

[*The MOTHER is lying down, "dead", before the audience, her eyes open*]

Suzanne's Voice: As often happens in the evening, a strange breeze from the Pacific came up and blew over the plain, over the mother's body, and was lost in the forest. Everything went dark. Night had fallen very suddenly, as it does in those parts. The forest had turned blue. Joseph came just after nightfall. He went in to our mother. We both stood looking at her for a long time.

[*Sound of a very strong wind. Of waves*]

[*And then everything goes dark*]

[*JOSEPH arrives at the same time as the darkness*]

[*He goes slowly over to the MOTHER*]

[*SUZANNE doesn't move*]

[*JOSEPH bends down, touches the MOTHER and lays his face against her*]

[*He straightens up and looks at her*]

Suzanne: His eyes were full of dull, mauve shadows. His mouth.... His hands. His northern peasant's hands. His hands...

[*Noises around the bungalow. Peasants arriving*]

The peasants came up from the plain and gathered around the bungalow.

[*Music*]

On the road, in a car, the woman from the Eden Cinema waited for Joseph.

[*The whole stage is motionless*]

[*JOSEPH leaves the MOTHER, comes and faces the audience*]

[*Silence. Then he speaks:*]

Joseph: The house is open to you all from now on. Come in. Take everything. I leave you my guns. Do what you like with them.

[*Pause*]

You can go in and see her if you like: the children as well.

Suzanne's Voice: One of the peasants asked me if we were going away for good. Joseph looked at me, he said yes.

[*Pause*]

[*Music*]

[*Pause*]

Joseph: We'll take her body far away. She was not of your race. Even though she loved you, even though her hope was your hope and she mourned the children of the plain, she was not of your race. She was always a stranger in your country.

[*Pause*]

All of us were always strangers in your country. She'll be buried in the French Cemetery in Saigon.

[*Everyone goes out except the CORPORAL who remains squatting beside the MOTHER*]

[*Children's laughter. Distant drums*]

[*Music*]

THE END.

Savannah Bay

[handwritten notes:] Silent trauma of the dead mother. Seperate to the trauma of the 2 characters.

repetition.
Fading + changing memory.
Recollection of memory changes the truth. Evolving, unfinish.

Characters

MADELEINE

YOUNG WOMAN

◇

An almost empty stage. In the foreground a table, with six chairs and two benches swathed in dust-sheets. Bare floor. All this occupies only a tenth of the total stage area, but it is here that Savannah Bay *will be enacted.*

Behind the foreground area and separate from it is a large set designed to suggest a vast empty landscape. A pair of curtains – wood painted to represent red velvet – are parted to reveal a central vista stretching as far as the back wall of the theatre. This central space is flanked first by a pair of huge bright-yellow marble pillars rising right up to the roof, then by a lofty dark-green double door, flung open and resembling the door of a cathedral in the Po valley. Through the opening lies first a band of almost black light, then the sea. The sea, which reflects a changing light now cold, now scorching and now sombre, is framed, like the scroll of the Law.

Thus the setting of Savannah Bay *is separate from the representation of* Savannah Bay – *uninhabitable by the women who are its protagonists; apart.*

Scene One

Edith Piaf is heard singing "Les Mots d'amour," very loud. As the fourth verse ends, MADELEINE appears in the shadows, emerging from the set. The YOUNG WOMAN soon follows, and joins her. They stand in the shadows and listen to the song. It fades. They speak.

Madeleine: What is it?

Young Woman: A record. For you. *forcing the past*

[*They both listen*]

Young Woman: Do you recognise it?

Madeleine: [*Hesitating*] Mmm...Yes... I think so.

[*The song continues, MADELEINE still following it intently*]

Madeleine: Who's the singer?

Young Woman: She's dead.

Madeleine: Oh.

Young Woman: She died about fifteen years ago.

Madeleine: [*Listening*] You'd think she was still here.

[*Pause*]

Young Woman: She is [*Pause*] You must have sung that song by the Magra... Several summers.

Madeleine: Yes, perhaps... perhaps.

Young Woman: [*Firmly*] You did. *Pursuing the past forcefully*

Madeleine: [*Listening*] She's very good.

Young Woman: Yes [*Pause*] The record was in the house for ages. And then it got broken.

Madeleine: [*Just breathing it*] Yes...

[*Pause. The music gets fainter. MADELEINE points towards its source*]

The singer... did I know her?

Young Woman: The name wouldn't mean anything to you.

Madeleine: No.

[*Pause*]

Young Woman: Do you recognise the voice?

Madeleine: Not the voice itself... Something in it... Its strength perhaps. It's very strong.

Young Woman: It's your strength. Your voice.

Madeleine: [*Not listening*] She killed herself, that woman.

Young Woman: [*Hesitating*] Yes. [*Pause*] You knew.

[*Pause*]

Madeleine: No. I just said it at random. [*Pause*] Perhaps the song suggests it.

[*Silence. The disc ends. The YOUNG WOMAN goes and fetches the tea things. MADELEINE sits*]

For months *I* died every night on the stage. Month after month, every night. [*Pause*] At a time of great sorrow.

[*Silence*]

Young Woman: I'll sing the tune and you say the words.

[*MADELEINE makes a wry face*]

Young Woman: Don't you want to?

Madeleine: Yes... Yes... All right [*Pause. She looks at the YOUNG WOMAN. Then suddenly, as if surprised*] Who are you? [*Pause*] A little girl? [*Pause. MADELEINE stands up. Afraid*] I can never quite remember...

[*The YOUNG WOMAN comes and stands in front of her*]

Young Woman: Look at me. I come to see you every day.

Madeleine: Of yes, of course. We play cards, don't we? Tell stories...?

Young Woman: That's right. And have tea. All sorts of things.

[*Pause*]

Madeleine: Yes... and one day... it's you who got me to count... That's it... numbers.

Young Woman: Yes.

Madeleine: Large numbers... huge...

Young Woman: That's right.

Madeleine: I know you now. [*Long pause*] You're the daughter of the child that died. Of my daughter that died. [*Long pause*] You're the daughter of Savannah. [*Pause. She shuts her eyes and caresses the empty air*] Yes... Yes... that's it. [*Her hands drop away from the head she has been stroking and fall to her sides despairingly*] I'd like to be left alone.

[*The YOUNG WOMAN comes and sits facing her*]

Young Woman: Look at me.

[*She starts to hum the tune, slowly*]

[*MADELEINE looks at her like a schoolchild looking at its teacher, and says the words slowly, without punctuation, as though they were being dictated*]

Madeleine: "I'm mad about you

Crazy about you
Sometimes I could cry aloud"

Young Woman: Yes.

[*Pause. Then she goes on with the tune, more slowly*]

Madeleine: [*More and more intent*]
"Never before
Have I loved like this
Never, I swear."

Young Woman: That's it.

[*Pause. Then she goes on again*]

Madeleine: [*Still without expression*]
"If you ever went,
went and left me..."

Young Woman: Yes [*Continues with tune*]

Madeleine: [*Still expressionless at first*] "I think I'd die".

[*Then, transfixed, as if stunned by the violence of the words:*] No.

Young Woman: [*Speaking, not singing*]
"If you ever went,
went and left me,
I think I'd die..
Die of love...
My love, my love."

Madeleine: No.

[*Pause*]

Young Woman: "I think I'd die."

Madeleine: "I think I'd die."

Young Woman: "Die of love...
My love, my love."

Madeleine: [*Meekly*] "Die of love..
My love, my love."

Young Woman: Yes.

[*The YOUNG WOMAN hums the song again and MADELEINE still listens with passionate attention. The YOUNG WOMAN stops to speak some of the words of the song*]

Young Woman: "Never before

    Have I loved like this..."

[*She hums the next few bars. Then, very deliberately, speaks*]

    It's you I love most in all the world. [*Pause*] More than anything.
    [*Pause*] More than anything I've ever seen. [*Pause*] Ever read.
    [*Pause*] More than anything I possess. [*Pause*] More than anything.

Madeleine: [*Bewildered but natural, accepting*] Me.

Young Woman: Yes.

[*Silence*]

[*MADELEINE, regal, primitive, does not try to understand. The YOUNG WOMAN looks at her as we ourselves might*]

Madeleine: Why do you tell me this today?

[*Pause*]

Young Woman: [*Cautiously*] What's special about today?

Madeleine: [*Looking around as if embarrassed*] I'd decided to ask
    that people shouldn't come to see me so often... Well... not quite
    so often...

[*Silence. Apologetic smile*]

Madeleine: I want to be here by myself. [*Sweeping gesture*] Alone.
    [*Then in a sudden shout*] I don't want anyone to come any more.

Young Woman: [*Gently*] Yes.

Madeleine: [*A complete change, to plaintiveness, love*] But you – what
    will become of you without me? [*Silence. She shuts her eyes, calls
    to someone else*] My baby, my child, my pretty one – didn't it want
    to live, then? Didn't it want to live? No, it didn't want anything.
    Anything at all.

[*The YOUNG WOMAN seems deliberately not to have heard. MADELEINE has spoken into some distant space in time*]

[*Silence*]

Young Woman: [*Hums the first verse of the song again, then speaks it
    as if in answer to Madeleine*]

    "I love you madly

    I'm crazy about you

    Sometimes I could cry aloud –"

Madeleine: [*In the past*] Yes.

[*Silence*]

Young Woman: I meant to tell you – I saw a photograph of those
    days – the time of the song. Everyone outside the boat-house.
    [*Pause*] There's a young girl.

[*Pause*]

Madeleine: There are always girls in holiday snaps.

[*Pause*]

Young Woman: There's a man on her right. Tall. Young, like her.
Holding her hand. [*Silence*] Then, later on, there's a photo of a
woman. With her hands over her face. Weeping. [*Pause*] It's a
scene from a play.

Madeleine: It's me. Me – in the theatre.

[*Silence. The YOUNG WOMAN gazes at MADELEINE*]

Young Woman: [*Fiercely*] Sometimes I don't recognise your voice.

Madeleine: That can happen, I believe.

Young Woman: [*Gently*] You don't understand much of what's said
to you now.

Madeleine: Yes, only a little. [*Pause*] Nothing at all, sometimes.

Young Woman: [*Slowly*] And sometimes everything.

Madeleine: Sometimes everything.

[*Silence*]

Young Woman: [*Gently*] One day, one evening, I shall leave you for
ever. I'll shut the door [*She points to it*], and it will be over. I'll kiss
your hands. Shut the door. It will be over.

Madeleine: [*Ritually*] Someone will come every evening to see. And
switch on the lamps?

Young Woman: Yes. [*Pause*] And one day there'll be no more light.
There'll be no more need.

[*Silence*]

Madeleine: That's right. They'll listen. And the breathing will have
stopped?

Young Woman: Yes.

[*Silence. MADELEINE looks at YOUNG WOMAN*]

Madeleine: And you – where will you be?

Young Woman: Gone. Different. For ever different. For ever without
you.

Madeleine: Without me? Without whom?

Young Woman: You. Without you.

[*They drink their tea*]

[*Pause*]

Madeleine: Death will come from outside me.

Young Woman: From far away. [*Pause*] You won't know when.

Madeleine: No. I shan't know.

Young Woman: It set out when the world began, in search of just you.

Madeleine: Yes. I was enrolled at birth. Before I was born. What an honour.

Young Woman: Yes.

Madeleine: [*Indicating the stage*] Just to get here. [*Pause*] How do you know these things?

Young Woman: I can see you.

[*Silence. The YOUNG WOMAN looks intently at MADELEINE. They drink their tea*]

Young Woman: You think all the time...all the time...about just one thing.

Madeleine: [*Matter-of-fact*] Yes.

Young Woman: [*Fiercely*] What? Can't you say what it is for once?

Madeleine: [*She is fierce too*] Find out for yourself!

Young Woman: You think about Savannah.

Madeleine: Yes. I imagine so.

[*Silence. They grow gentle again*]

Young Woman: Savannah comes with the speed of light. Goes with the speed of light. No time for words any more.

Madeleine: No. No time.

Young Woman: And at any moment. Unpredictable.

Madeleine: Unpredictable as happiness.

[*Silence. The YOUNG WOMAN goes over to MADELEINE and points to her own dress*]

Young Woman: Look – it's the costume you wore in that film – *Journey to Siam.*

Madeleine: Yes... so it is... It suits you... It really does...

[*The YOUNG WOMAN takes MADELEINE over to an invisible mirror, a patch of burning light. They both gaze at MADELEINE's "reflection"*]

Young Woman: Look at yourself...

[*Silence*]

Madeleine: [*Very simply*] I think I look lovely.

Young Woman: I think so too. Lovely.

[*Silence*]

Madeleine: Red still suits me... and then the dress too...

[*She inspects it, turning to and fro in front of the mirror*]

Young Woman: Where's it from?

Madeleine: [*With a gesture*] The wardrobe room. I got it out this morning.

Young Woman: You wore it in lots of productions.

Madeleine: Oh yes. Excellent shows. Tragedies...comedies... All sorts.

Young Woman: Yes...of course. [*Pause*] You were an actress, weren't you?

Madeleine: [*As if just finding it out*] Yes... yes... an actress. That's what I was.

Young Woman: An actress...

Madeleine: A theatre actress.

[*Pause*]

Young Woman: And that was all.

Madeleine: That was all.

[*The YOUNG WOMAN prowls round MADELEINE*]

Young Woman: Tell me the story again.

Madeleine: Every day you ask for it.

Young Woman: Yes.

Madeleine: And every day I end up making mistakes... in the dates... the people... the places...

[*They both suddenly laugh*]

Young Woman: Yes.

Madeleine: And that's what you want?

Young Woman: Yes.

[*They laugh. Then the laughter dies away*]

Scene Two

The action begins. The setting is gradually sketched in .

Young Woman: A big white rock, surrounded by sea.

Madeleine: Flat. The size of a room.

Young Woman: Splendid as a palace.

Madeleine: As the sea. Like the sea.

Young Woman: It broke off the mountain when the sea swept in.

Madeleine: And remained there. Too heavy to be washed away.

[*Pause*]

Young Woman: With the grain of the sea. Of the water.

Madeleine: And with the rough shape of the wind.

[*Silence*]

Impossible to speak of it.

Young Woman: We do speak of it. [*Pause. Slowly*] It was summer.

Madeleine: Summer. By the sea.

Young Woman: You're not sure of anything any more.

Madeleine: I'm not sure of much. [*Pause*] The white rock – I'm sure of that. [*Pause*] You had to swim out to it. It had fallen into the sea. [*Pause*] It was there they met, on that big flat patch surrounded by sea...

Young Woman: Almost awash. Whenever a boat went by the swell covered it, covered the rock with cool water. Then the sun came back and in a few seconds made it scorching hot again.(*Pause*) It was summer. The school holidays. She was very young. Just out of high school. She used to swim a long way out.

Madeleine: Sometimes...for a minute or so... you might have thought she wasn't coming back. But she did. For a long while she did.

Young Woman: It was there they met. It was there he saw her, lying on the rock, smiling, washed over every so often by the swell.

[*Pause*]

Madeleine: She'd taken the short cut round by the marshes. He'd come along the path by the river. It was nearly noon.

Young Woman: It was a very hot spell. You've forgotten.

Madeleine: No. I remember. It was a very hot spell, the hottest of the summer.

Young Woman: [*With a gesture*] When he reached the mouth of the river and saw the sea, where the rock is, he saw her. A little black-clad shape on the white of the rock. [*Long pause*] Then he saw her jump in the sea and swim away.

Madeleine: Cleaving the sea with her body. Disappearing in an eddy. The water closed up over her.

Young Woman: There's nothing more to be seen on the surface. [*Pause*] So he shouts. [*Pause*] Suddenly he stands up on the white rock and shouts. That he wants to see her again – the girl in the black swimsuit. [*Pause*] And she hears and comes back.

Madeleine: But it isn't easy. She's too light for the dense rough water. My child.

Young Woman: And when he saw her coming back...he smiled...and that smile...

Madeleine: [*Distrait, not listening*]...is terrible, not to be looked at... it makes you think... that for once... even if only for an instant... you might... it might be possible... to die of love.

[*Silence*]

I think it was in Montpellier, between 1930 and 1935. At the local theatre. A new author. French, I think.

[*Silence*]

At that time, and in the years that followed, I was on stage somewhere every night. Everywhere. All over the world. [*Pause*] You might have thought I was acting different parts. But in fact I was acting only the one. Through all that people thought I was acting, I was acting the story of the white rock. [*Long pause*] Do you begin to understand?

Young Woman: Yes. [*Pause*] Are you play-acting deliberately?

Madeleine: Yes.

Young Woman: Are you lying?

[*Silence*]

No, you're not lying

Madeleine: No.

[*Pause*]

Young Woman: [*Gently*] She was wherever you were.

Madeleine: She was wherever I was.

[*Pause*]

Young Woman: She was there before she was born, too.

Madeleine: Yes. Before she was born.

Young Woman: Yes. [*Pause*] In those theatres, shut in there with you, all over the world.

Madeleine: All over the world.

Young Woman: And then came that summer day.

[*They both avert their faces, cover them with their hands, but with no sign of weeping either in their voices or their eyes*]

Young Woman: My love.

Madeleine: Yes. [*Pause*] My love, my treasure, my precious. Precious.

[*Silence*]

I can remember, but it's lost its shape, it's hidden. I can't remember what I remember when I remember her. But it's there.

[*Silence*]

Young Woman: I won't ever leave you.

Madeleine: [*Still distrait, not listening*] My love, my little one...

Young Woman: Yes. [*Pause*] What does the story say?

Madeleine: That it was when she laughed that you might have thought she was there. That she would still stay.

Young Woman: Not every one thinks that. Some say death was already there in her laughter. A light, easy laugh. Like air.

Madeleine: People say that?

Young Woman: Yes.

[*Pause*]

What do *you* say?

Madeleine: I say that when she laughed –

[*She comes to a painful halt. Then starts to stare at the YOUNG WOMAN*]

Young Woman: [*Leading her out of her pain*] She wore a black swimsuit.

Madeleine: [*Repeating it after her*] She wore a black swimsuit.

Young Woman: Very slim...

Madeleine: Very Slim.

Young Woman: Very fair.

Madeleine: I don't remember. [*She goes over to the YOUNG WOMAN, touches her face, scrutinizes the colour of her eyes*] The eyes – I remember them – blue or grey according to the light. By the sea they were blue. [*Silence*] Between her and him there's this blue, this expanse of rough sea, very deep, very blue.

[*Pause*]

Young Woman: He goes to the water's edge and takes her by the arms. [*Pause*] Pulls her out of the sea.

Madeleine: Takes her hands and draws her to him. Her skin burns, cracks, when he takes her hands and draws her out of the sea.

[*Silence*]

Young Woman: He has taken her out of the sea. [*Pause*] Laid her down on the rock and looked at her. [*Long pause*] He gazes at her. Seems astonished. [*Pause*] She rests after her swim, lets herself be washed over by the swell, breathes betweenwhiles, shuts her eyes.

Madeleine: He takes her by the shoulders, lifts her up, draws her suddenly out of the swell, kisses the closed eyes and calls to her. [*Pause*] Those kisses...those kisses...God...He didn't know her, didn't know her name. He calls her by other names. Including Savannah.

Young Woman: She opens her eyes. Sees him. [*Lomg pause*] They stay like that for a long while, seeing each other. [*Long pause*] For the first time they see each other. See and are seen. As far as the eye can.

Madeleine: And then he speaks to her,

Young Woman: He speaks [*with a gesture*]...right into her face.

Madeleine: He speaks as he looks – not thinking of her.

Young Woman: He says what people usually say.

Madeleine: What people always say before they meet...touch...take. [*Pause*] Maybe he said he was surprised to see her there, of all places, so far from all he'd known. So different.

Young Woman: And *you* – where are *you?*

Madeleine: I stayed at home, in the dark, the shutters closed because of the heat. The house is gloomy, stifling. I know she's gone out to the white rock.

[*Pause*]

Young Woman: You can hear what they say.

Madeleine: Yes. The wind.

Young Woman: It carries their voices.

Madeleine: Yes. The wind from the river carries their voices.

[*Pause*]

Young Woman: He takes her head in his hands, holds it in his arms out of the sun, speaks. [*Pause*] He says, "Aren't you tired, swimming all that way? How do you manage it? Be careful of the sun. It's terrible here – you don't seem to realise."

Madeleine: She says, "I'm used to the sea."

Young Woman: He says no, it's not possible. Ever. She says no. Never. [*Silence*] He says. "I don't know how to look at you. It's not that you're beautiful. It's something else, more mysterious, more terrible. I don't know what."

Madeleine: She says, "No, I don't know what it is, what you're talking about, either. I've never been so close to a man. I'm sixteen."

Young Woman: They leave the white rock. Very slowly they swim along by the sands. And suddenly he shuts his eyes so as not to see her. Swims fast so as to leave her behind. Then comes back. Says, "I've come back."

[*Silence*]

Madeleine: It's then she says. "I can be yours if you like. I will if you want. I'm old enough, and look – there's no one here to see. We're at the mouth of the Magra." [*Long pause*] He asks: "Why are you making up to me?"

Young Woman: She says it's just a manner of speaking. She doesn't know anything about such things yet. She spoke at random.

[*Pause*]

Madeleine: He says: "Very well. Be mine. But I'm afraid, and I wish you'd tell me why."

Young Woman: She smiles. "I've always had a strange desire inside me. A wish to die. I use the word for want of a better, but perhaps you guessed what I meant because of the awkward way I asked. And maybe that's why you're afraid."

Madeleine: He asks: "Did you choose me because I'm afraid?"

Young Woman: She says: "Yes, probably. But I'm not sure. I don't understand the thing I'm talking about. I don't know the kind of fear it inspires."

Madeleine: "But you speak of death."

Young Woman: "Yes, I speak of the fear the word inspires, but that doesn't mean I understand the thing itself. Or that I can express the unknown element in it, the simultaneous fear and attraction. And this inability is part of the strange reason I told you about – the wish to die."

Madeleine: "Do you know anything about death?"

Young Woman: She smiles, says, "Nothing, yet, but the life from which it comes." [*Silence*] They've reached the stretch of marshes around the Magra. Here the sea breeze drops. Here the sounds of summer and all movement fade away. Nothing but reeds and the nests of sea-birds.

Madeleine: She says: "This is where I've always wanted to be."

[*Pause*]

Young Woman: She says: "If you like we can love each other. [*Pause*] Here I'm not afraid of dying any more."

[*Silence*]

Madeleine: The sky of the room has gone dark. Their shadows have vanished from the walls.[*Pause*] I forget.

[*Long silence. Sound of Schubert's String Quintet*]

Madeleine: I have all the doors in the house opened – the door on the Magra, the door of the boathouse, the doors of the bedrooms... So that everything may sweep in and slay... The marshes, the mud, the river... It was such a mighty love...

[*They both shut their eyes and remain motionless. The adagio. A moment's repose. Then the YOUNG WOMAN takes MADELEINE over to mirror, and very slowly, as the music continues, places a number of necklaces round her neck. MADELEINE is passive. Helps the young woman as she carefully adorns her. Smiles. When all the necklaces are on, the YOUNG WOMAN puts her arms around MADELEINE as if MADELEINE were her own child, and addresses her with a kind of passionate love*]

Young Woman: [*With a smile of great tenderness*] My little girl... my daughter... my poppet... my treasure... my darling... my love... my little one.

Madeleine: [*Echoes her*] My little one... my precious. [*Pause. Then, ringingly*] It was a hot spell. [*Pause*] Bright. [*Pause*] Very very bright. [*Pause*] Full of people on holiday, full of light. [*Pause*] Full of boats, large and small. Of joy.

Young Woman: [*Also in a ringing voice*] Full of cries and laughter. [*Pause*] Of singing. [*Pause*] And of the sea. [*Pause*] Of blue.

Madeleine: Full of cool shade. Of sun. Of the white of the rock.

Young Woman: Of her. [*Pause*] Of the white of the rock and of her against the white. [*Silence*] She laughs. Cries out that her skin is burning, scorching against his. And her takes her arms and draws her out of the water like an eel, and she lets him and lies down on the rock, and stretches out her body and her heart and her whole self and skin on the burning rock.

Madeleine: And he takes off her black swimsuit, and she is naked, bare, and he covers her with kisses, her whole body, belly, heart, eyes.

[*Silence. Dying echo of the brightness*]

Madeleine: Someone weeps with happiness to see them.

Young Woman: Someone weeps with happiness because they're going to die of love. [*Silence*] The child.

Madeleine: The child started to cry when night fell. Everyone was distracted by suffering, and had forgotten it.

Young Woman: A little girl? [*Pause*] Was she hungry?

Madeleine: [*Smiling*] Yes...yes... a little girl...she was hungry.

[*Silence. The YOUNG WOMAN takes MADELEINE for a long stroll. First upstage, to the door on the sea, a sort of altar opening on the ocean, on the light. This light darkens or grows coldly incandescent according to the fierceness or gentleness with which the two women summon up the memory of the girl who died in the warm sea of Savannah Bay. Then the stroll brings them nearer, to the curtains and the pillars. The whole thing takes four or five minutes. They do not speak. After looking out to sea they look at their surroundings, then stop and look at the auditorium, the audience. All the time they are walking about, the Piaf song is being played on the piano*]

Scene Three

Young Woman: And then one day nothing happened. [*Pause*] One day it was rainy and dull. [*Pause*] All day long. [*Pause*] The sky had disappeared – the light, the air, the trees. Night fell fast. [*Pause*] The lights were lit. No one spoke. [*Pause*] Who died that dull day? [*Long pause*] Who died that dull day? You've never said. You've never said anyone did die. Why not her? [*Pause*] Why not her? The irreplaceable one – why shouldn't she be dead like the rest?

[*Silence*]

[*MADELEINE looks at her, terrified*]

You've always spoken of an interminably long day – a day that lasted a hundred years. You said the house was darkened. That everything was silent except for the man calling. Don't you remember?

Madeleine: No.

Young Woman: What *do* you remember?

Madeleine: The great stretch of marshes at the mouth of the Magra. The woods. They're still there. [*Pause*] The sea. [*Pause*] The rock. [*Pause*] The weather.

Young Woman: The cries.

Madeleine: No. The story.

[*Pause*]

Young Woman: There'd never been such a love?

Madeleine: No.

[*Silence*]

Young Woman: What was it like?

Madeleine: A love...[*Pause*] A love belonging to every moment. [*Pause*] Without a past. [*Pause*] Without a future. [*Pause*] Changeless. [*Pause*] A crime.

[*Silence*]

Young Woman: The sun every morning emerging from the dark, and they loving each other with a love that is total, fatal, in that unvarying weather.

Madeleine: Yes. In the unvarying weather, that...strange...love.

[*Silence*]

Young Woman: Is that what people said? And later someone wrote a book about it?

Madeleine: I think so. A play, too. And then a film. [*Pause*] But the film was later, much later. The film was all about him. [*Pause*] I found out he was still alive. I met him in a town in Siam. At Savannah Bay. [*Silence*] A little girl was born then, wasn't she? During the days you say were...so terrible?

[*Pause*]

Young Woman: A little girl was born that day – yes. The day of the death. [*Pause*] Here the memory's clear and bright. It was in the paper, don't you remember? She was supposed to have got up from her confinement and gone to the marshes...

Madeleine: Oh yes... got up from her confinement and gone to the marshes. [*Pause*] That's what they said. I believe she was very much criticised for that – for leaving the child.

[*Pause*]

Young Woman: The child – perhaps that was too much happiness all at once? [*Pause*] Perhaps the child was unnecessary. [*Pause*] Perhaps their love left no room for any other. [*Pause*] Perhaps nothing could have prevented the death. [*Pause*] It was the end of the summer, wasn't it? Night? Raining?

[*Pause*]

Madeleine: Night. Raining. It ofter rained there at the end of the summer. [*Pause*] She had left her mother too. [*Silence*] They wanted nothing between the two of them. They wanted an empty world and themselves alone in it. [*Pause*] For them the days didn't need to be different any more, it didn't need to be winter or summer. [*Long pause*] In the play, yes, the man called out from the marshes... "Listen ...someone's shouting ... it's coming from the marshes ... Listen." [*Long pause*] No one went to see. [*Pause*] Someone had left a back door open. He could have come back. But he didn't. [*Pause*] Perhaps he's forgotten the way...Perhaps ...But admittedly we'd forgotten how to talk, how to weep, everything. [*Pause*] I don't know if they ever found the body. I never asked. [*Pause*] I don't remember. [*Silence. She tries to remember, can't be sure*] Perhaps it was one of the men on the white rock... the one she chose, to love and to die.

[*Silence*]

Young Woman: On the third day...

Madeleine: On the third day, when the sun rose, there was no more shouting. Not anywhere. [*Pause*] Who knows? Perhaps he chose to live...to go away. [*Long pause*] Strange... That kind of thing I *am* sure of...the dark. [*Pause*] The rain. [*Pause*] The cries. [*Pause*] The sunrise the next morning. [*Pause*] The colour of the sea...[*Pause*] The sound of voices. [*Pause*] The silence between the voices. [*Long pause. Absently*] He called out to her over the sea: "Savannah." Sometimes he shouted it, sometimes he said it very softly. No one understood. [*Pause. Angrily*] How can anyone be expected to understand people like that, who speak only to each other when they're face to face with eternity?

[*Silence*]

Young Woman: Someone might have called them...

Madeleine: Someone might have called them... begged them to come back. But no one did... Apparently... It concerned the lovers alone... [*Pause. Slowly*] They must have swum a long way out. It was her idea. That's certain. And then... it must have been like falling asleep. [*Long pause*] It must have been easy for her, she was so tired... she'd been confined that night... For him, no, it must have been impossible. His strength was unimpaired, he couldn't have cast it off and stopped himself from swimming. [*Pause*] That's what people said, and wrote, and acted. Everywhere.

Young Woman: [*Her face hidden*] And what do you say?

Madeleine: [*Decidedly, as if delivering a verdict*] I say it was a moment, the way the rock is white. No one there any more. All of a sudden.

Young Woman: Just the sea around the rock. [*Pause*] The cries.

[Silence] A moment in a play.

Madeleine: A moment of infinite pain.

[The YOUNG WOMAN goes over to MADELEINE, who remains sitting by the table. The Schubert comes to an end]

Young Woman: The theatre's full. You keep from dying out of politeness. The audience is waiting. It has a right to the show.

Madeleine: The theatre's dark. *[Pause]* You tell it who died. *[Pause]* Who's still alive. *[Pause]* Who shouted. *[Pause]* You tell it the sea was blue. *[Pause]* How hot it was. *[Pause]* How white the rock.

Young Woman: How long the pain. *[Pause]* How it changes. *[Pause]* What it becomes. *[Pause]* The second journey. *[Pause]* The other shore. *[Pause]* The second love.

Madeleine: The second love.

[The door on the sea lights up. The light all around the two women changes. MADELEINE turns and looks at the door opening on to the light. Stands there, gazing. The YOUNG WOMAN goes over to the door and stands for a while on the brink of the light. She puts her hand to her brow and scans the sea. Then comes quietly back to MADELEINE, takes a scarf and puts it over her shoulders. As though it will soon be night. They are close to one another. The music is loud, sometimes almost fading out but lasting till the end of the play]

Young Woman: No one would write that play for you?

[Pause]

Madeleine: No, never. For very commonplace reasons. *[Pause]* Didn't want to revive the pain, you know. And then I couldn't rush about any more, throwing myself at them... and then taking myself off. *[Pause]* You see the kind of thing...

Young Woman: Didn't we hear a song?

Madeleine: Yes. "*My Love, My Love.*" Do you know it?

Young Woman: Yes.

[Silence]

[Sudden gaiety]

Madeleine: The play will never be written. So might as well die.

Young Woman: Or might a well live

Madeleine: Mm. I suppose so.

Young Woman: So it's a play that has never been performed, never even written.

Madeleine: No. That play, never. *[Pause]* Or rather, it will never have been performed completely. *[Pause]* But in the theatre nothing is ever really performed completely...And so...You think you're acting one thing and you're acting another. I've seen great actors suddenly mistake the play they're in.. .and no one noticed. [*Pause*] In the theatre everything connects with everything else. Every play with every other. But nothing is ever truly performed. You always act as if it were possible to...to... But...

Young Woman: Possible to do what?

Madeleine: Well...to say...[*With sublime simplicity*]: "Good morning, madame, good morning...this weather is enough to make you want to die, isn't it madame... of too much light...of the blue of the sky...or even of love. Isn't it, madame? Good morning, madame..."

Young Woman: Good morning, good morning...

[*They laugh lightheartedly. Then stop. They return to the table and take up their cups of tea again*]

Young Woman: In the theatre, too, you met him again in a town in Siam, didn't you?

Madeleine: Yes. In a bar [*Pause*] I recognised him.

[*Pause*]

Young Woman: [*As if telling a story*] It's at the end of a day. [*Pause*] Just before nightfall. [*Pause*] When the light lengthens. [*Pause*] Luminous, before it fades.

Madeleine: Dusk. [*Pause*] You can't see where the sea ends. [*Pause*] The great expanse of the sea merges with the red expanse of the sky.

[*Silence*]

Young Woman: A man is weeping.

Madeleine: A man inconsolable for the loss of a woman. [*Pause*] I love him like that, bereft of the object of his love – as I'd have loved my own lover. As soon as I see him I feel a great desire for his body, bereft of her. [*Pause*] I weep, so great is the desire. [*Pause*] His eyes are pale.

[*Silence*]

[*Suddenly we are in Siam*]

Young Woman: Do you live in Siam, madame?

Madeleine: Well, sometimes, monsieur, you see, I forget where I... I'm so sorry.

Young Woman: She's here to make a film. She's in a film being made in Savannah Bay, with Henry Fonda.

Madeleine: [*Happily*] Yes, that's right. I'm in a film being made in Savannah Bay with Henry Fonda. It's called *Savannah Bay.*

Young Woman: They often come here to make films. Because of the marvellous light in Savannah Bay.

Madeleine: Marvellous...marvellous...

Young Woman: Always the same. It hardly ever rains. Maybe a few hurricanes around the equinox. That's all.

Madeleine: That's all.

[*Pause*]

Young Woman: A love story, madame?

Madeleine: Of course, monsieur.

[*Music. Schubert*].

[*MADELEINE wipes away a couple of tears with her finger*]

Young Woman: Why are you suddenly so sad, madame?

Madeleine: [*Slowly*] "Because...I forget what I'm weeping for, monsieur" [*Silence*] If you ask me, monsieur, she killed herself here one night, here on this very spot. Savannah Bay. Dead for love. [*Silence*] You might have been her lover. [*Pause*] She could have tried to take you with her. [*Pause*] But you couldn't manage to die. [*Pause*] She'd have been seventeen. [*Pause*] There'd have been a child born of that love. [*Pause*] Of that death in the warm sea of Savannah Bay. But who knows? [*Long Pause*] That's what I think I once knew. [*Long pause*] But it must have been a long time ago, monsieur. Years and years. [*Pause*] And so I mix up the dates, monsieur,...the people ...the places...[*Pause*] Everywhere, she's dead.]*Pause*] Everywhere, she's born. [*Pause*] Everywhere she dies at Savannah Bay. [*Pause*] And is born there. At Savannah.

Young Woman: He said it wasn't him she'd loved. [*Pause*] "I'm not the one, madame. I'm sorry."

Madeleine: "It's of no consequence, monsieur. No consequence." [*Silence*] I was leaving. Going away from Siam.

Young Woman: Starting to search again.

Madeleine: Yes. Everywhere. In all the cities in the world that are beside the sea.

Young Woman: Shanghai. Calcutta. Rangoon. [*Pause*] And other places... [*Pause*] Bombay... Paris – Prague... Bangkok... Djakarta... Singapore... Lahore... Biarritz... Sydney...

Madeleine: Saigon... Dublin... Osaka... Colombo... Rio... [*Pause*]And who knows? [*Pause*] Who knows?

[*Silence. The tone changes, as if belonging to another time*]

Young Woman: Did I tell you? – the child that was born wasn't given a name.

Madeleine: She gave herself a name, later.

Young Woman: That's right. She called herself Savannah.

[*Pause*]

The name of fire.

Madeleine: The name of the sea.

THE END

India Song

CHARACTERS

Anne-Marie Stretter
The Beggar Woman
Michael Richardson
The Young Attaché (not named)
The Stretters' Guest (not named)
George Crawn
The French Vice-Consul in Lahore (not named)
Servant 1
Servant 2

| 10 extras, women. | 2 women's voices |
| 10 extras, men. | 2 men's voices. |

GENERAL REMARKS

The names of Indian towns, rivers, states and seas are used here primarily in a musical sense.

All references to physical, human or political geography are incorrect: You can't drive from Calcutta to the estuary of the Ganges in an afternoon. Nor to Nepal. The Prince of Wales hotel is not on an island in the Delta, but in Colombo. And New Delhi, not Calcutta, is the administrative capital of India. And so on.

The characters in the story have been taken out of a book called *The Vice-Consul* and projected into new narrative regions. So it is not possible to relate them back to the book and see *India Song* as a film or theatre adaptation of *The Vice-Consul*. Even where a whole episode is taken over from the book, its insertion into the new narrative means that it has to be read, seen, differently.

In fact, *India Song* follows on from *The Woman of the Ganges*. If *The Woman of the Ganges* hadn't been written, neither would *India Song*. The fact that it goes into and reveals an unexplored area of *The Vice-Consul* wouldn't have been a sufficient reason.

What was a sufficient reason was the discovery, in *The Woman of the Ganges*, of the means of exploration, revelation: the voices external to the narrative. This discovery made it possible to let the narrative be forgotten and put at the disposal of memories other than that of the author: memories which might remember, in the same way, any other love story. Memories that distort. That create.

Some voices from *The Woman of the Ganges* have been used here. And even some of their words.

That is about all that can be said.

As far as I know, no *India Song* yet exists. When it has been written, the author will make it available and it should be used for all performances in *India Song* in France and elsewhere.

If by any chance *India Song* were performed in France, there should be no public rehearsal. This does not apply to other countries.

NOTES ON VOICES 1 AND 2

Voices 1 and 2 are women's voices. Young. They are linked together by a love story. Sometimes they speak of this love, their own. Most of the time they speak of another love, another story. But this other story leads us back to theirs. And vice versa.

Unlike the men's voices - Voices 3 and 4, which don't come in until the end of the narrative - the women's voices are tinged with madness. Their sweetness is pernicious. Their memory of the love story is illogical, anarchic. Most of the time they are in a state of transport, a delirium, at once calm and feverish. Voice 1 is consumed with the story of Anne-Marie Stretter. Voice 2 is consumed with its passion for Voice 1.

They should always be heard with perfect clarity, but the level varies according to what they are saying. They are most immediately present when they veer towards their own story - i.e. when, in the course of a perpetual shifting process, the love story of *India Song* is juxtaposed with their own. But there is a distinction. When they speak of the story we see unfolding before us, they rediscover it at the same time as us, and so are frightened and perhaps moved by it in the same way as we are. But when they speak of their own story, they are always shot through with desire, and we should feel the difference between their two passions. Above all, we should feel the terror of Voice 2 at the fascination the resuscitated story exerts over Voice 1. Voice 1 is in danger of being "lost" in the story of *India Song*, which is in the past, legendary, a model. Voice 1 is in danger of departing its own life. The voices are never raised, and their sweetness remains constant.

NOTES ON VOICES 3 AND 4

Voices 3 and 4 are men's voices. The only thing that connects them is the fascination exerted on them by the story of the lovers of the Ganges, especially, once again, by that of Anne-Marie Stretter. Voice 3 can remember almost nothing of the chronology of the story. It questions Voice 4, and Voice 4 answers. Of all the voices, Voice 4 is the one which has forgotton the story the least. It knows almost all of it. But voice 3, although it has forgotten almost everything, recognises things as Voice 4 relates them. Voice 4 doesn't tell it anything it didn't know before, at a time when it too knew the story very well. The difference between Voices 3 and 4, between forgetfulness on the one hand and remembrance on the other, arises from the same cause - the fascination the story exerts on the two voices. Voice 3 has rejected the fascination, Voice 4 has tolerated it. The story of the lovers of the Ganges is *in* both voices - latent in the one, manifest in the other. About to survive or revive. The difference - between the tolerable and the intolerable - should be reflected in the sensibilities of the two voices. It is not without apprehension that Voice 4 informs Voice 3. Voice 4 hesitates. For Voice 3 is exposed to the danger, not of madness, like Voice 1, but of suffering.

I

[*A tune from between the two wars,* India Song, *is played slowly on the piano. It is played right through, to cover the time - always long - that it takes the audience, or the reader, to emerge from the ordinary world they are in when the performance, or the book, begins.* India Song *still. Still. And now it ends. Now it is repeated, farther away than the first time, as if it were being played elsewhere. Now it is played at its usual rhythm - blues. The darkness begins to lighten. As the dark slowly disperses, suddenly there are voices. Others besides ourselves were watching, hearing, what we thought we alone were watching and hearing. They are women. The voices are slow, sweet. Very close, enclosed like us in this place. And intangible, inaccessible.*]

Voice 1: He followed her to India.

Voice 2: Yes.

[*Pause*]

Voice 2: For her he left everything. Overnight.

Voice 1: The night of the dance?

Voice 2: Yes.

[*The light continues to grow. We still hear* India Song. *The voices are silent for some time. Then they begin again*]

Voice 1: Was it she who played the piano?

Voice 2: [*Hesitating*] Yes...but he played too. It was he who used sometimes, in the evening, to play the tune they played in S. Thala...

[*Silence*]

[*A house in India. Huge. A "white people's" house. Divans. Armchairs. Furniture of the period of* India Song. *A ceiling fan is working, but at nightmare slowness. Net screens over the windows. Beyond, the paths of a large tropical garden. Oleanders. Palm trees. Complete stillness. No wind outside. Inside, dense shadow. Is it the evening? We don't know. Space. Gilt. A piano. Unlit chandeliers. Indoor plants. Nothing moves, nothing except the fan, which moves with nightmare "unreality". The slowness of the voices goes with the very slow growth of the light; their sweetness matches the poignancy of the setting*]

Voice 1: [*As if reading*] "Michael Richardson was engaged to a girl from S. Thala. Lola Valerie Stein. They were to have been married in the autumn. Then there was the dance. The dance at S. Thala..."

[*Silence*]

Voice 2: She arrived at the dance late... in the middle of the night...

Voice 1: Yes... dressed in black... What love, at the dance... What desire...

[*Silence*]

[*As the light grows we see, set in this colonial decor, presences. There were people there all the time. They are behind either a row of plants, or a fine net screen, or a transparent blind, or smoke from perfume-burners - something which makes the second part of the space explored less easily visible. Lying on a divan, long, slender, almost thin, is a woman dressed in black. Sitting close to her is a man, also dressed in black. Away from the lovers there is another man in black. (One of the men is smoking a cigarette - is that what made us sense there were people there?)*]

[*VOICE 1 discovers - after we do - the presence of the woman in black*]

Voice 1: [*Tense and low*] Anne-Marie Stretter...

[*It is as if VOICE 2 had not heard*]

Voice 2: [*Low*] How pale you are... What are you frightened of...

[*No answer*]

[*Silence*]

[*The three people seem struck by a deathly stillness.* India Song *has stopped. The voices grow lower, to match the deathliness of the scene*]

Voice 2: After she died, he left India...

[*Silence*]

[*That was said all in one breath, as if recited slowly. So the woman in black, there in front of us, is dead. The light is now steady, sombre. Silence everywhere. Near and far. The voices are full of pain. Their memory, which was gone, is coming back. But they are as sweet, as gentle as before*]

Voice 2: She's buried in the English cemetery...

[*Pause*]

Voice 1: ... she died there?

Voice 2: In the islands. [*Hesitates*] One night. Found dead.

[*Silence*]

[India Song *again, slow, far away. At first we don't see the movement, the beginnings of movement. But it begins exactly on the first note of* India Song. *The woman in black and the man sitting near her begin to stir. Emerge from death. Their footsteps make no sound. They are standing up. They are close together. What are they doing? They are dancing. Dancing. We only realize it when they are already dancing. They go on, slowly, dancing. When VOICE 1 speaks they have been dancing for some time. VOICE 1 is gradually remembering*]

Voice 1: The French Embassy in India....

Voice 2: Yes.

[*Pause*]

Voice 1: That murmur? The Ganges?

Voice 2: Yes.

[*Pause*]

Voice 1: That light?

Voice 2: The monsoon.

Voice 1: ...no wind...

Voice 2: ...it will break over Bengal...

Voice 1: The dust?

Voice 2: The middle of Calcutta.

[*Silence*]

Voice 1: Isn't there a smell of flowers?

Voice 2: Leprosy.

[*Silence*]

[*They are still dancing to* India Song. *They are dancing. But it needs to be said. (As if otherwise it weren't sure. And so that the image and the Voices coincide, touch)*]

Voice 2: They're dancing.

[*Silence*]

Voice 2: In the evening they used to dance.

[*Silence*]

[*They dance. So close they are one.* India Song *fades in the distance. They are merged together in the dance, almost motionless. Now quite motionless*]

Voice 2: Why are you crying?

[No answer]

[Silence]

[No more music. A murmur in the distance. Then it stops. Other murmurs. They, the man and woman, are still motionless in the silence hemmed in by sound. Fixed. Arrested. It lasts a long while. Over the fixed couple:]

Voice 2: I love you so much I can't see any more, can't hear...can't live...

[No answer]

[Silence]

[India Song *comes back from far away. Slowly the couple unfreeze, come back to life. Sound increases behind the music: the sound of Calcutta: a loud, a great murmur. All around, various other sounds. The regular cries of merchants. Dogs. Shouts in the distance. As the sound outside increases, the sky in the garden becomes overcast. Murky light. No wind]*

[Silence]

[The couple separate and turn towards the garden. They look out at it, motionless. The second man sitting there also begins to look out at the garden. The light grows still murkier. The sound of Calcutta ceases. Waiting. Waiting. It is almost dark. Suddenly the waiting is over. The noise of the rain. A cool, slaking noise. It is raining over Bengal. The rain cannot be seen. Only heard. As if it were raining everywhere except in the garden, deleted from life. Everyone looks at the sound of the rain]

Voice 2: *[Scarcely voiced]* It's raining over Bengal...

Voice 1: An ocean...

[Silence]

[Cries in the distance, of joy, shouts in Hindustani, the unknown language. The light gradually returns. The rain, the noise, very loud for a few seconds. It grows less. Isolated shouts and laughter are heard more clearly through the sound of the rain. The light continues to grow stronger. Suddenly, clearer, nearer cries - a woman's. Her laughter]

Voice 1: Someone's shouting... a woman...

Voice 2: What?

Voice 1: Disconnected words. She's laughing.

Voice 2: A beggar.

[Pause]

Voice 1: Mad?

Voice 2: Yes...

[*In the garden paths, sun after the rain. Moving sunlight. Patches of light, grey, pale. Still shouting and laughter of the beggar women*]

Voice 1: Oh yes... I remember. She goes by the banks of the rivers. Is she from Burma?

Voice 2: Yes.

[*While the voices speak of the beggar, the three people move, leave the room by side doors*]

Voice 2: She's not Indian. She comes from Savannakhet. Born there.

Voice 1: Ah yes... yes... One day... she's been walking ten years, and one day, there in front of her, the Ganges?

Voice 2: Yes. And there she stops.

Voice 1: Yes...

[*The three people have disappeared. The place is empty. Someone is speaking, almost shouting, in the distance, in a soft-sounding language, Laotian*]

Voice 1: [*After a pause*] Twelve children die while she's walking to Bengal...?

Voice 2: Yes. She leaves them. Sells them. Forgets them. [*Pause*]. On the way to Bengal, becomes barren.

[*The three people reach the garden and stroll slowly through the cool after the rain, moving through the patches of sunlight. In the distance, the shouting of the beggar woman, still. Suddenly, in the shouting, the word Savannakhet. The voices halt briefly. Then resume:*]

Voice 1: Savannakhet - Laos?

Voice 2: Yes. [*Pause*] Seventeen... she's pregnant, she's seventeen. [*Pause*] She's turned out by her mother, goes away. [*Pause*] She asks the way to get lost. Remember? No one knows.

Voice 1: [*Pause*] Yes, one day, she's been walking ten years, and one day: Calcutta, there in front of her. She stays.

[*Silence*]

Voice 2: She's there on the banks of the Ganges, under the trees. She has forgotten.

[*Silence*]

[*The three people go out of the garden. Movements of light, monsoon, in the empty garden. The song of the beggar - "song of Savannakhet" - in the distance. (VOICE 2 is informative, calm, gentle)*]

Voice 2: Lepers burst like sacks of dust, you know.

Voice 1: Don't suffer?

Voice 2: No. Not a thing. Laugh.

[*Silence*]

Voice 2: They were there together, in Calcutta. The white woman and the other. During the same years.

[*The voices are silent. A distant part of the garden, so far very dark, as if neglected by the lighting, gradually becomes visible. It is revealed by spotlights - extremely slowly, but regularly, mathematically. Far away, the song of Savannakhet - coming, going. Sound of Calcutta, in the distance*]

[*The wire netting round a tennis court emerges from the darkness. Against the wire a woman's bicycle - red. The place is deserted. The voices recognize these things and are afraid*]

Voice 1: [*Smothered exclamation of fear*] The tennis courts, deserted...

Voice 2: [*The same*]... Anne-Marie Stretter's red bicycle...

[*Silence*]

[*A man has come into the garden. Tall, thin, dressed in white. He walks slowly. His footsteps make no sound. He gazes around him at the stillness everywhere. Gazes for some time. Tries to see into the house: no one there. Now what is he looking at? We don't know at first. Then it becomes clear: he's looking at Anne-Marie Stretter's red bicycle by the deserted tennis courts. He goes over to the bicycle. Stops. Hesitates. Doesn't go any nearer. Looks, stares at it. (The voices are low, scared)*]

Voice 2: ... he comes every night...

[*Pause*]

Voice 1: The French Vice-Consul in Lahore.

Voice 2: Yes. ...in Calcutta in disgrace...

[*Silence*]

[*Slowly, the man in white moves. He walks. He goes along a path. He goes away. Disappears. After he has disappeared, everything remains in suspense. Silence. Fear. The song of Savannakhet, in the distance, innocent*]

[*Then two shots. The first makes the light go dim. The second makes it go out*]

[*Silence*]

[*Blackout*]

[*The song of Savannakhet stopped when the shots were fired. As if they had been aimed at it*]

[*Silence. Blackout*]

[*The voices are very quiet, terrified*]

Voice 2: Someone fired a gun under the trees... on the banks of the Ganges...

[*Silence*]

Voice 1: It was a song of Savannakhet...?

Voice 2: Yes.

[*Silence*]

[*By a strictly symmetrical inversion, and without passing through any intermediate stages, the light becomes the same as it was when the first shot made it go dim. This stands for night. It is night. The place, the stage, is still empty. The only movement - that of the nightmare fan. Time passes over the empty place*]

[*Silence*]

[*A Hindu servant dressed in white goes by, passing through the drawing-rooms of the French Embassy. He has gone. Emptiness again. Far away, the song of Savannakhet begins again: the beggar woman wasn't killed. The voices are still low, frightened*]

Voice 1: ... she's not dead...

Voice 2: Can't die.

Voice 1: [*Scarcely heard*] No...

[*Silence*]

Voice 2: She goes hunting at night beside the Ganges. For food...

[*No answer*]

[*Silence*]

Voice 1: Where's the one dressed in black.

Voice 2: Out. Every evening. She comes back when it's dark.

[*Silence*]

[*A servant enters, lights a lamp, very faint, in a corner of the room. Does various things. Goes away (but remains visible). Comes back. Opens a window. Perhaps he lights some sticks of incense against the mosquitoes - in which case the audience will be able to smell it. Empties ashtrays*]

Voice 2: She's back. The Embassy's black Lancia has just come through the gates.

[*Silence*]

[The servant goes out. The place remains empty for a few more seconds, and then the woman in black enters the darkness. She is bare-foot. Her hair is loose. She is wearing a short wrap of loose black cotton. The scene is very long and slow. Slowly she goes and stands under the nightmare fan. Stays there. Puts up her hands and thrusts her hair away from her body in a gesture of exhaustion - someone stifling from the heat. Then lets her arms fall down by her sides. Through the opening of the wrap, the white of the naked body. She freezes. Head thrown back. Gasping for air. Trying to escape out of the heat. Touching grace of the thin, fragile body. Stays like that, upright, exposed. Offered to the "voices" (The voices are slow, stifled, a prey to desire - through this motionless body)]

Voice 2: *[Smothered outburst]* How lovely you look dressed in white...

[Pause]

Voice 1: I'd like to go and visit the woman of the Ganges...

[Held pause]

Voice 1: ...The white woman...

Voice 2: *[Pause]* The one who...?

Voice 1: Her...

Voice 2: ... dead in the islands...

Voice 1: Eyes dead, blinded with light.

Voice 2: Yes. There under the stone. In a bend in the Ganges.

[Silence]

[Still motionless before us, the dead woman of the Ganges. The voices are a song so quiet it does not awaken her death. Apparently nothing changes, nothing happens. But suddenly, fear]

Voice 1: *[Low frightened]* What is it?

[No answer]

Voice 1: *[As before]* What time is it?

Voice 2: *[Pause]* Four o'clock. Black night.

[Pause]

Voice 1: No one can sleep?

Voice 2: No.

[Silence]

[Tears on the woman's face. The features remain unmoving. She is weeping. Without suffering. A state of tears. The voices speak of the heat, they speak of desire - as if the voices are issuing from the weeping body]

Voice 1: The heat. Impossible. Terrible.

[*Pause*]

Voice 2: Another storm... Approaching Bengal...

Voice 1: [*Pause*] Coming from the islands...

Voice 2: [*Pause*] The estuaries. Inexhaustible...

[*Silence*]

Voice 1: What's that sound?

Voice 2: [*Pause*] Her weeping.

[*Silence*]

Voice 1: Doesn't suffer, does she...?

Voice 2: She neither. A leper, of the heart.

[*Silence*]

Voice 1: Can't bear it...?

Voice 2: No. Can't bear it. Can't bear India.

[*Silence*]

[*A man enters through the door on the left. He too is wearing a black wrap. He halts, looks at her. Then slowly goes over to her, a statue in her tears under the fan, asleep. He looks at her - asleep standing up. Goes right up to her. Passes lightly over her face a hand outspread in a caress. Takes his hand away, looks at it: it is wet from the tears*]

Voice 2: [*Very low*] She's asleep.

[*With infinite precaution, the man takes up the weeping woman and lays her down on the floor. He's the man we have already seen, the man she danced with at the dance in S. Thala: MICHAEL RICHARDSON. He sits down beside the outstretched body. Looks at it. Uncovers the body so that it is better exposed to the cool - imaginary - from the fan. Strokes her forehead. Wipes away the tears, the sweat. Caresses the sleeping body. Doesn't go close. Stays there watching over her sleep. The voices slow down to the rhythm of the man's movements, taking up again in a sort of sung complaint the themes adjacent to the main story*]

Voice 1: He loved her more than anything in the world.

Voice 2: [*Pause*] More even than that...

[*Silence*]

[*VOICE 2 spoke as if of its own love*]

Voice 1: Where was the girl from S. Thala?

[*No answer*]

Voice 1: [*As if reading*] "From behind the indoor plants in the bar, she watches them. [*Pause*] It was only at dawn...[*Stops*]... when the lovers were going towards the door of the ballroom that Lola Valerie Stein uttered a cry."

[*Silence*]

[*In the distance, a regular cry in Hindustani. Someone selling something again. It stops. Quiet*]

Voice 2: At four in the morning, sometimes sleep comes.

[*Silence*]

[*The lover is still beside the sleeping body. He looks at it. Takes the hands, touches them. Looks at them. They fall back, dead*]

[*Silence*]

Voice 1: She never got over it, the girl from S. Thala?

Voice 2: Never.

Voice 1: They didn't hear her cry out?

Voice 2: No. Couldn't hear any more. Couldn't see.

[*Pause*]

Voice 1: They abandoned her? [*Pause*] Killed her?

Voice 2: Yes.

[*Pause*]

Voice 1: And with this crime behind them.

Voice 2: [*Scarcely heard*] Yes.

[*Silence*]

Voice 1: What did the girl from S. Thala want?

Voice 2: To go with them. See them. The lovers of the Ganges: to see them.

[*Silence*]

[*That is what we are doing: seeing. Slowly the man lies down beside the sleeping body. His hand goes on caressing the face, the body. Far away, distant sounds, oars, water. Then laughter, a zither, fading in the distance. Then it stops*]

Voice 2: Listen... Ganges fishermen... Musicians...

[*Silence again. The voices speak of the heat again. Of their desire*]

Voice 2: [*Very slow*] What darkness. What heat. Unmitigated. Deathly.

[*Silence*]

[*A voice that is clear, implacable, terrifying:*]

Voice 2: I love you with a desire that is absolute.

[*No Answer*]

[*Silence*]

[*The hand of MICHAEL RICHARDSON - the lover - immediately stops caressing the body, as if interested by what VOICE 2 has just said. It lies there where it is on the body*]

[*Silence*]

[*A second man enters the room. He stands in the doorway for a moment, looking at the lovers. MICHAEL RICHARDSON's hand starts to move again, caressing the uncovered body. The man goes over to them. Like the lover, he sits down beside her. The lover's hand now moves more slowly. Then it stops. The newcomer does not caress the woman's body. He lies down too. All three lie motionless under the fan*]

[*Silence*]

[*Rain*]

[*Another storm over Bengal. The sound of rain over sleep. The voices are like breaths of coolness, gentle murmurs*]

Voice 1: ...rain...

Voice 2: Yes...

[*Pause*]

Voice 1: ...cool...

[*Silence*]

[*The sky gets lighter, but it is still night. Gradually, music: Beethoven's 14th Variation on a Theme of Diabelli. Piano, very distant. The rain slackens. In its place, a white light. Patches of moonlight on the garden paths. No wind. The three bodies, their eyes closed, sleep. The voices, interwoven, in a climax of sweetness, are about to sing the legend of ANNE-MARIE STRETTER. A slow recitative made up of scraps of memory. Out of it, every so often, a phrase emerges, intact, from oblivion*]

Voice 1: Venice. She was from Venice...

Voice 2: Yes, the music was in Venice. A hope in music...

Voice 1: [*Pause*] She never gave up playing?

Voice 2: No.

[*Silence*]

Voice 1: [*Very slow*] Anna Maria Guardi...

Voice 2: Yes.

[*Silence*]

Voice 1: The first marriage, the first post...?

Voice 2: Savannahket, Laos. She's married to a French colonial official. She's eighteen.

Voice 1: [*Remembering*] Ah yes... a river... she's sitting by a river. Already... Looking at it.

Voice 2: The Mekong.

Voice 1: [*Pause*] She's silent? Crying?

Voice 2: Yes. They say: "She can't get acclimatized. She'll have to be sent back to Europe."

[*Pause*]

Voice 1: Couldn't bear it. Even then.

Voice 2: Even then.

[*Silence*]

Voice 1: [*Visionary*] Those walls all round her?

Voice 2: The grounds of the chancellery.

Voice 1: [*As before*] The sentries?

Voice 2: Official.

Voice 1: Even then...

Voice 2: Yes.

Voice 1: Even then, couldn't bear it.

Voice 2: No.

[*Silence*]

Voice 2: One day a government launch calls. Monsieur Stretter is inspecting the posts on the Mekong.

Voice 1: [*Pause*] He takes her away from Savannahket?

Voice 2: Yes. Takes her with him. Takes her with him for seventeen years through the capitals of Asia.

[*Pause*]

Voice 2: You find her in Peking. Then in Mandalay. In Bangkok. Rangoon. Sydney. Lahore. Seventeen years. You find her in Calcutta. In Calcutta: she dies.

[*Silence*]

[*The tall thin man dressed in white enters the garden. The voices haven't seen him. He stops. Looks through the screens on the windows at the three sleeping forms. Stops, looking at her, the woman. The voices still haven't seen him*]

Voice 1: Michael Richardson used to go to S. Thala in the summer.

Voice 2: Yes. She didn't go often. But that summer....

Voice 1: He was English, Michael Richardson?

Voice 2: Yes. [*Pause. As if reading*] "Michael Richardson started a marine insurance company in Bengal, so that he could stay in India."

Voice 1: Near her.

Voice 2: Yes.

[*The man goes away. We see him, from behind, going slowly along the path towards the deserted tennis courts*]

Voice 1: The other man who's sleeping?

Voice 2: Passing through. A friend of the Stretters'. She belongs to whoever wants her. Gives her to whoever will have her.

Voice 1: [*Pause. Pain*] Prostitution in Calcutta.

Voice 2: Yes. She's a Christian without God. Splendour.

Voice 1: [*Very slow*] Love.

Voice 2: [*Scarcely heard*] Yes...

[*Silence*]

[*The thin man goes towards the red bicycle propped against the wire round the deserted tennis courts. The voices have seen him. They resume very softly, in fear*]

Voice 1: He's back in the garden.

Voice 2: Yes... Every night... Looks at her...

[*Silence*]

[*The man hesitates. Then goes up to ANNE-MARIE STRETTER's bicycle*]

Voice 1: He never spoke to her...

Voice 2: No. Never went near a...

[*Halt*]

Voice 1: The male virgin of Lahore...

Voice 2: Yes...

[*The man is beside the bicycle. Puts out his hands. Hesitates. Then touches it. Strokes it. Leans forwards and holds it in his arm. Stays clasping ANNE-MARIE STRETTER's bicycle - frozen in this gesture of desire*]

[*Silence*]

[*Almost imperceptibly, a movement over by the sleeping bodies. It is her. As he bends over the bicycle, she, by a converse movement, sits up. In the same slow rhythm she sits up and turns towards the garden. ANNE-MARIE STRETTER looks at the man in white with his arms round her bicycle*]

[*Silence*]

[*Suddenly the man lets go of the bicycle. Remains with his arms hanging by his sides, his hands open, in an attitude of passion and despair. Sound of a man sobbing (the only sound heard directly). The woman still looks, sitting with her hands flat on the ground. The sobs cease. The man gets up. He stands facing the bicycle. Then slowly turns round. Sees her. The woman doesn't move*]

[*Silence*]

[*They look at each other. This lasts several seconds*]

[*Silence*]

[*It is the man who stops looking. First he turns his face away. Then his body moves. He walks away. She, still sitting, watches him walk away. Then, after he has slowly disappeared from sight, she takes up her former position, asleep under the nightmare fan*]

[*Silence*]

[*Stillness. Sobs of the VICE-CONSUL in the distance. Silence again. In the garden the light grows dim again, murky. No wind in the deserted garden*]

Voice 2: [*Afraid, very low*] The sound of your heart frightens me...

[*Silence*]

[*Another stirring in the still mass of the three sleeping bodies: MICHAEL RICHARDSON's hand reaches out to the woman's body, caresses it, stays there. MICHAEL RICHARDSON was not asleep. The light gets dimmer still. VOICE 2 is full of desire and terror*]

Voice 2: Your heart, so young, a child's.

[*No Answer*]

[*Silence*]

Voice 2: Where are you?

[*No Answer*]

[*Silence*]

[*Shouts in the distance: the VICE-CONSUL. Cries of despair. Heartrending, obscene*]

Voice 1: [*Distant*] What's he shouting?

Voice 2: The name she used to have in Venice, in the desert of Calcutta.

[*Silence*]

[*The cries fade in the distance. Disappear. VOICE 2, all in one breath, in fear, tells the story of the crime, the crime committed in Lahore*]

Voice 2: [*Low*] "He fired a gun. One night, from his balcony in Lahore, he fired on the lepers in the Shalimar gardens."

[*Silence*]

[*VOICE 1 is gentle - calm and gentle*]

Voice 1: Couldn't bear it.

Voice 2: No.

Voice 1: India - couldn't bear India?

Voice 2: No.

Voice 1: What couldn't he bear about it?

Voice 2: The idea.

[*Silence*]

[*It is getting darker. The bodies grow less and less distinguishable. Above them the fan goes on turning, the blades gleaming slowly. You can no longer tell one body from another*]

[*Silence*]

Voice 1: A black Lancia is speeding along the road to Chandernagor...

[*No answer*]

Voice 1: [*Continuing*] ... it was there... there that she first...

[*The voice stops*]

Voice 2: Yes. Brought back by ambulance. They talked about an accident...

[*Pause*]

Voice 1: She's been thin ever since.

Voice 2: [*Scarcely heard. Continuing*] Yes.

[*Beethoven's 14th Variation on a Theme of Diabelli. Distant*]

[*Total Blackout*]

[*Then, beyond the garden, gleams in the sky. Either day or fire - rust coloured fire. The voice is slow: a calm consideration*]

Voice 1: Those gleams over there?

Voice 2: The burning-ghats.

Voice 1: Burning people who've starved to death?

Voice 2: Yes. It will soon be daylight.

[*Silence*]

[*The 14th Variation is heard till the end, over the gleams from the burning-ghats*]

[*Blackout*]

II

We are in the same place as before. The only difference is that the right side of it is now revealed, as if the angle of vision had been changed. Doors opening on the reception rooms on one side, and on the other on the garden. (As if these rooms were in a wing of the Embassy). Bright light everywhere. Chandeliers. Chinese lanterns in the garden. Silence. It was as if the French Embassy were quite empty. Nothing can be seen of the reception rooms except the light coming out of the doors and illuminating the garden. All remains empty for a few seconds. Then, without a sound, a servant passes through. Carrying a tray with glasses of champagne, he goes through and out towards the right. Silence again. Emptiness again. Waiting. Then, suddenly noise. The noise of the reception begins quite suddenly, full volume. The party is triggered off as if by some mechanism: the noise bursts forth instantaneously from behind the walls, through the open doors. A woman is singing "The Merry Widow", accompanied by a piano and two violins. Behind the music, the sound of many conversations all merging into one. The sound of glasses, crockery, etc. But the feet of the dancers make no sound.

No conversation will take place on the stage, or be seen. It will never be the actors on the stage who are speaking. The only exception to this rule is that the sobs of the French VICE-CONSUL are both seen and heard. When the conversations recorded here take place, the sound of the reception grows fainter. Often it <u>almost</u> stops: for example, during the conversations between the YOUNG ATTACHÉ and ANNE-MARIE STRETTER, and between her and the French VICE-CONSUL. It is as if the guests at the reception, intrigued, watched them talking instead of talking themselves. So the fading of the sound is not arbitrary. All the conversations, whether private or not, whether they make the guests around them go quiet or not, should give the impression that only the spectators hear them clearly - not the guests. So the sound of the reception should be heard, however faintly, behind all the conversations. The fact that these conversations are now and again mingled with conversations on other subjects should prove that the private *conversations are not audible, or hardly, to the guests. So also the fact that some of what is overheard is sometimes repeated, but always more or less wrongly - with slight mistakes which show that only the spectators hear the private conversations properly. The sound of the reception should come from the right and from the stage and from the auditorium, as if the reception was taking place beyond the walls of the auditorium, too. ANNE-MARIE STRETTER wears a black dress - the one she wore at the dance in S. Thala - the one described in LE RAVISSEMENT DE LOLA V. STEIN. The men wear black dinner jackets, with the exception of the French VICE-CONSUL in Lahore, who wears a white one. The other women at the reception wear long dresses, coloured. The reception overflows, all the time it lasts, either into the garden or into the place we already know: ANNE-MARIE STRETTER's private drawing-room. From the point-of-view of sound, the image, the stage, plays the part of an echo-chamber. Passing through that space, the voices should sound, to the spectator, like his own "internal reading" voice. The set should seem accidental - stolen from a "whole" that is by its nature inaccessible, i.e. the reception. The diction should in general be extremely precise. It should not seem completely natural. During rehearsals some slight defect should be settled on, common to all the voices. One ought to get the impression of a reading, but one which is reported, i.e. one which has been performed before. That is what is meant by an "internal reading" voice. To repeat: not a single word is uttered on the stage]*

["Heure Exquise" sung by a woman. Then repeated by the orchestra. A waltzing couple cross a corner of the garden]

Some women are talking: *[Quite close]*

This is the last reception before the monsoon.

What? Do you mean to say the monsoon hasn't begun?

Not really. It'll be at its height in a fortnight. No sun for six months... You'll see... No one can sleep... They just wait for the storms to break...

[An Indian servant passes through, on his way to the reception. He carries a tray with brimming glasses of champagne. Two couples go through, waltzing. Slowly. Disappear]

Some women are talking: *[Farther away]*

She invited the French Vice-Consul in Lahore...

Yes. At the last minute she sent him a card: "Come". The Ambassador didn't say anything.

[A young man arrives. He stops and looks around. Clearly he isn't familiar with this part of the Embassy. He looks tired, as if he wants to get away from the reception. He looks out towards the deserted tennis courts. As he looks, a couple dance across a corner of the garden and

disappear]

Some men are talking: [*About the young man*]

Who is he?

The new Attaché... Only been out here a month. He can't get used to it.

It's the first time he's been here.

[*Pause*]

He'll be back. He'll be invited, he'll go to the islands... The Ambassador asks people to stay there. For her - for his wife.

[*Pause*]

What makes you think he'll be asked?

[*Pause*]

He looks so troubled... She doesn't like people who get used to it.

Are there any?

Some...

Clubs, to keep India out, that's the answer... isn't it?

Yes.

[*The YOUNG ATTACHÉ goes on looking around. Then he turns towards the dancing, watches the reception. And goes back to it. "Heure Exquise" ends. There is a moment without music. Only the sound of the reception. No laughter. A sort of general dejection. Some women go by in the garden, looking curiously towards ANNE-MARIE STRETTER's drawing room. They fan themselves with big white fans. They are gone*]

A man speaks: [*The Ambassador*]

I think my wife may have mentioned it... we'd be very glad if you'd join us some time in the islands... There are some newcomers one feels specially attracted to... And the rules governing ordinary society don't apply here... We don't choose... [*A smile in the voice*] You will? The Residency looks out on the Indian Ocean, it dates from the days of the Company, it's worth seeing. And the islands were very healthy, especially the main one, it's the biggest island in the Delta.

[*Silence*]

Men:

He used to write, the Ambassador... Did you know? I've heard a little volume of his poems.

So I've heard... They say it's because of her he gave it up...

[*"Heure Exquise" has been followed by a tango. The French VICE-CONSUL in Labore has come into the garden. He is wearing a white dinner-jacket. He is alone. No one seems to have noticed him yet*]

Two conversations: [*1 and 2*] [*Between men and women*]

No.1: She might have spared us the embarrassment...

[*Pause*]

>   What exactly did he do? I never know what goes on...

>   The worst possible thing... How can I explain...?

>   The worst...?

[*Silence*]

No.2:   An intriguing woman. No one really knows how she spends her time... What does she do? She must do something....

>   She must read... Between her siesta and when it's time to go out, what else could she do...

>   Parcels of books come for her from Venice... And she spends some time with her daughters... In the dry season they play tennis - you see all three of them going by the office, dressed in white...

[*Pause*]

>   The fact that one wonders what she does, that's what's strangest of all.

[*Silence*]

No.1: [*Continued*]

>   Did he kill somebody?

>   He used to fire shots at the Shalimar gardens at night...

>   You knew that? ... But bullets were found in the mirrors of his own residence in Lahore...

>   He was shooting at himself... [*Little laugh*]

[*No answer*]

>   It's difficult to tell which are the lepers...

>   You see, you do know: you talk about the lepers...

[*Silence*]

No.2: [*Continued*]

>   She goes cycling too, very early in the morning, in the grounds. Not during the monsoon, of course...

No.1: [*Continued*]

>   What's the official version?

>   His nerves gave way... Often happens.

[*Pause*]

>   Funny, he forces you to think about him.

[*MICHAEL RICHARDSON has entered. He is not wearing a dinner jacket. He sits down. He smokes a cigarette. He doesn't look towards the garden. In the garden, the VICE-CONSUL: he looks at MICHAEL RICHARDSON. Two women enter on the right, and stop. They see MICHAEL RICHARDSON, and look at him with curiosity. He doesn't see them. A servant goes by with glasses of champagne. He offers one to MICHAEL RICHARDSON, and goes. The tango, as if in the distance. MICHAEL RICHARDSON gets up, begins to go towards the reception, looks at it from some distance, then turns round: sees the VICE-CONSUL in the garden. Then the women see him too and draw back*]

Women: [*Low*]

Look... Michael Richardson...

[*Pause*]

Yes... He doesn't attend receptions?

No, only at the end, towards the middle of the night. When there's just a few friends left...

[*Pause*]

What a business...what love... They say he gave up everything to be with her...

Everything. He was engaged to be married. Everything. Overnight.

[*Silence*]

[*MICHAEL RICHARDSON makes a movement towards the VICE-CONSUL - towards the gate into the garden. The VICE-CONSUL turns away. MICHAEL RICHARDSON stops. The two women watch*]

Women: [*Low, afraid*]

Look in the garden...

Is that him?

Yes.

So thin... and the face... as if it were grafted on... so pale...

[*Silence*]

[*MICHAEL RICHARDSON turns back towards the reception. The watching women disappear.*]

Women: [*Continued*]

Do they know each other?

Evidently not...

[*Silence*]

[*The VICE-CONSUL looks at the reception. MICHAEL RICHARDSON looks again at him. The VICE-CONSUL seems absorbed, and does not notice him*]

Men:

He used to fire shots at night from his balcony.

Yes. He used to shout too. Half naked.

What?

Disconnected words. He used to laugh.

[*Pause*]

And no woman was ever close enough to him, in Lahore, to be able to say anything...?

No. Never.

How is that possible?

His house, no one ever went to his house in Lahore...

It's terrifying... Such abstinence... Terrible...

[*Silence*]

[*MICHAEL RICHARDSON turns towards the reception, tries to make out what the VICE-CONSUL can be watching so avidly*]

Men and women:

Did you hear? The Ambassador said to the Young Attaché: "People avoid him, I know... he frightens them. But I'd be grateful if you'd go and have a word with him."

[*Pause*]

What's known about his background? His childhood?

His father was a bank manager in Neuilly. An only child. The mother's supposed to have left father. Expelled from several schools for bad behaviour. Brilliant at his work, but after high school... That's all.

So they don't know anything about him really?

Nothing.

[*Pause*]

Isn't there in all of us... how shall I put it?... a chance in a thousand we might be like him... I mean... [*Pause*]. I'm only asking.

[*No answer*]

[*Silence*]

[*A couple come to the edge of the garden. They see the VICE-CONSUL, and don't go any farther. MICHAEL RICHARDSON looks at them. They hesitate. Turn away. Go back to the reception. The VICE-CONSUL looks at the reception and laughs. Some women go through the garden*] *fanning themselves. They don't see the VICE-CONSUL. They stop and look at the reception from a distance: something catches their attention*]

Women:

Who's she dancing with?

The Ambassador.

You knew he took her away from some official in the wilds of French Indochina... I can't quite remember where... Laos, I think...

Savannakhet?

That's it...

Don't you remember?..."slow launch with... awnings, slow journey up the Mekong to Savannakhet... wide expanse of water between virgin forest, grey paddy-fields... and in the evening, clusters of mosquitoes clinging to the mosquito-nets..."

What a memory! [*Little laugh*]

[*Silence*]

Seventeen years they've been wandering round Asia.

[*Silence*]

[*They all look towards the reception, towards the Ambassador dancing with his wife. The VICE-CONSUL laughs silently*]

Men:

Has he talked to anyone about Lahore?

Never.

About anything else?

I don't think so... He gets letters from France. An elderly aunt... The letters were intercepted... Apparently... he told the secretary of the European Club he was in a reformatory school... when he was fifteen... in the North...

He talks to him, then? That drunk?

Well... the other one's asleep, so really he's talking to himself... [*Little laugh*]

So he doesn't talk to anyone then...

That's right... [*Little laugh*]

What did he find in India to set him off? Didn't he know about it before? Did he actually have to see it? It's not so difficult to find out...

Women:

There are moments when he seems happy. Look... As if he were suddenly madly happy...

[*Pause*]

Perhaps when she dances...

What an idea...

I've only just noticed...

[*Silence*]

Who mentioned Bombay?

He did, to the secretary at the Club. He saw himself being photographed beside the Sea of Oman on a chaise-longue... [*Little laugh*]

He doesn't talk about it any more, apparently.

[*Silence*]

[*The YOUNG ATTACHÉ has now entered the garden. He goes towards the French VICE-CONSUL, slowly, as if not to frighten him. The VICE-CONSUL makes as if to run away. The YOUNG ATTACHÉ hesitates, then takes him by the arm. The VICE-CONSUL doesn't attempt to run away any more. The YOUNG ATTACHÉ signals to the VICE-CONSUL to go with him. They go towards the reception. Go in. MICHAEL RICHARDSON has seen them - he is the only one not watching ANNE-MARIE STRETTER dancing with her husband*]

Women:

Did you see?...

[*Pause*]

Yes, it's her he's looking at....

[*Pause*]

If you ask me, Bombay's too popular, they'll send him somewhere else...

[*Silence*]

Tell me about Madame Stretter.

Irreproachable. Outside the kitchens you'll see big jars of cold water put out for the beggars... It's she who...

... Irreproachable... [*Little laugh*] come, come...

Nothing that shows. That's what we mean here by irreproachable.

[*Silence*]

[*Several people go into the garden and look towards the reception. Women fan themselves. (It is to be remembered that it's never those who are seen that speak)*]

A man and a woman:

She looks... imprisoned in a kind of suffering. But... a very old suffering... too old to make her sad any more...

[*Pause*]

And yet she cries... People have seen her... in the garden... sometimes...

The light perhaps, it's so harsh... and her eyes are so pale...

Perhaps... What grace... look....

Yes...

Frightening... don't you think?

[*Silence*]

[*MICHAEL RICHARDSON has sat down on the left side of the room. He looks as if he is waiting. He doesn't look towards the reception. He is clearly visible. Very handsome. Younger than ANNE-MARIE STRETTER. Obviously shy. He is smoking. He is tense, absorbed. Several conversations take place between people, some of whom have, and some of whom have not seen the VICE-CONSUL go into the reception*]

Women:

The roses are sent direct from Nepal...

She gives them away when the dance is over...

[*Low*] Look... There he is...

[*Silence*]

He doesn't notice everyone is looking at him...

You can hardly see his eyes...

His face looks dead... Don't you think so?... Frightening...

Yes. The laugh looks... stuck on... [*Pause*] What's he laughing at?

Who knows?

[*Pause*]

In the gardens, on the way to the office, he whistles *India Song*.

What work does he do?

Filing... nothing much... just to keep him occupied...

[*Silence*]

Men:

It's strange - most women in India have very white skins...

They live out of the sun. Closed shutters... they're recluses...

And they don't do anything out here... they're waited on.

Yes. They just rest.

[*Silence*]

I admit I have a look when she and her daughter go by on their way to play tennis... In shorts... Women's legs seem so beautiful here... walking through all that horror... [*Pause, then a start*] But look...

[*Silence*]

Women:

The first thing to see is the islands...

They're so beautiful... I don't know what we'd do here without them.

That's what we'll miss about India - the islands in the Indian Ocean...

[*Silence*]

Isolated woman's voice:

The best thing during the monsoon... did you know?... hot green tea, the way the Chinese make it...

[*Silence*]

Women:

Do you see? The Young Attaché talking to the Vice-Consul from Lahore...

[*Silence*]

The voice... listen to the voice... how blank it is....

[*Silence*]

[*Almost total silence. Everyone look at the YOUNG ATTACHÉ and the VICE-CONSUL. (The VICE-CONSUL's voice is harsh, almost strident. The YOUNG ATTACHÉ's voice is low and soft)*]

[*YOUNG ATTACHÉ and VICE-CONSUL*]

Vice-Consul: Yes, it's difficult, of course. But what is it with you, exactly?

Young Attaché: The heat, naturally. But also the monotony... the light... no colour. I don't know if I shall ever get used to it.

Vice-Consul: As bad as that?

Young Attaché: Well... I wasn't prejudiced before I left France... What about you? before Lahore? would you have preferred somewhere else?

Vice-Consul: No. Lahore was what I wanted.

[*Silence*]

[*Then* India Song]

Men and women: [*Low*]

Did you hear?

Not very clearly. I thought he said: "Lahore was what I desired"...

I heard: "What I... What I'd..."

And what does it mean? Nothing...

[*In one breath*] The report said people used to see him at night through his bedroom window, walking up and down as if it was broad daylight... and talking... always to himself... at night... as if it was daylight...

Yes...

[*Silence*]

[*One man's voice is heard dominating all the others*]

Man (George Crawn):

Come over to the bar. Allow me to introduce myself. An old friend of Anne-Marie Stretter's. George Crawn... Serve yourselves... there isn't a barman...

[*Hubbub for a few seconds - people going over to the bar*]

Woman:

He said that to distract people's attention.

[*The noise dies down*]

Young Attaché: Come over to the bar. [*Pause*] What are you afraid of?

[*No Answer*]

Young Attaché: They say you'd like to go to Bombay?

Vice-Consul: Won't they let me stay in Calcutta?

Young Attaché: No.

Vice-Consul: In that case I leave it to the authorities. They can send me where they like.

Young Attaché: Bombay's not so crowded, the climate's better, and it's pleasant to be by the sea.

[*Silence*]

Isolated man's voice:

It's as if he didn't hear when you speak to him.

Young Attaché: What are you doing? Come along...

Vice-Consul: I'm listening to *India Song*. [*Pause*] I came to India because of it.

[*ANNE-MARIE STRETTER appears on the stage for the first time in Act Two. She has come from the reception. She smiles at MICHAEL RICHARDSON. He stands, and watches her coming. He doesn't smile. No one sees them (Everyone is watching the VICE-CONSUL and the YOUNG ATTACHÉ). It was she that MICHAEL RICHARDSON was waiting for. ANNE-MARIE STRETTER and MICHAEL RICHARDSON look at each other. He puts his arms round her. They dance in a corner of the room, alone. We hear the public voice of the VICE-CONSUL*]

Vice-Consul: That tune makes me want to love. I never have.

[*No answer*]

[*Silence*]

[*The last speech was delivered while we could see the couple dancing. The couple disappear, left.* India Song *still*]

Vice-Consul: I'm sorry. I didn't ask to see my file. But you know it. What do they say?

Young Attaché: They say Lahore... What you did in Lahore... People can't understand it, no one can, no matter how they try...

Vice-Consul: No one?

[*No answer*]

[*Silence*]

[*The beggar woman appears in the garden. She hides behind a bush. Stays there*]

Men:

He said it was impossible for him to give a convincing explanation of what he did in Lahore.

...convincing...?

I was particularly struck by the word.

[ANNE-MARIE STRETTER comes back, from the left side of the room. Slowly. She stops. She looks towards the garden: the two women of the Ganges look at each other. The BEGGAR, unafraid, sticks her bald head out, then hides again. ANNE-MARIE STRETTER walks away, with the same slow step]

Women:

> She goes to the islands alone. The Ambassador goes hunting in Nepal.
>
> Alone... well...
>
> With him, Michael Richardson. And others...
>
> They say her lovers are Englishmen, foreigners from the embassies... They say the Ambassador knows...
>
> It's only what he expected when he met her... he's older than she is...

[Pause]

> There's a friendship between them now that's proof against anything...

[Silence]

[ANNE-MARIE STRETTER has gone into the reception. India Song ends. The VICE-CONSUL goes back into the garden. He is near the BEGGAR, but they don't see each other. A blues]

Men and women:

> Protocol requires everyone to have one dance with the Ambassador's wife...
>
> Look... He's left the Young Attaché... He's gone back into the garden...
>
> Again... Ever since the beginning of the evening he's kept going back there...
>
> As if he was on the point of running away.
>
> And yet at the same time...

[Silence]

[The VICE-CONSUL stands motionless, staring at the reception with all his might]

Men and Women: *[Continued]*

> What's he looking at?
>
> The Ambassador's wife dancing with the Young Attaché.

[Silence]

[*The YOUNG ATTACHÉ and ANNE-MARIE STRETTER dance into the room, then back to the reception. They too create a silence around them*]

Women: [*Low*]

Did you hear? [*Pause*]. She said to him: "I wish I were arriving in India for the first time during the summer monsoon." [*Pause*]. They're too far away... I can't hear any more...

[*Conversation between ANNE-MARIE STRETTER (voice marvellous in its sweetness) and the YOUNG ATTACHÉ*]

Anne-Marie Stretter: [*Deliberate repetition with slight error*] I wish I were you, coming here for the first time in the rains. [*Pause*] You're not bored? What do you do? In the evenings? On Sundays?

Young Attaché: I read... I sleep... I don't really know...

Anne-Marie Stretter: [*Pause*] Boredom is a personal thing of course. One doesn't know what to advise.

Young Attaché: I don't think I'm bored.

[*Pause*]

Anne-Marie Stretter: And then... [*Stops*]... perhaps it's not so important as people make out... Thank you for the parcels of books, you send them on from the office so quickly...

Young Attaché: A pleasure...

[*Silence*]

[*The noise gradually starts up around them again, faintly*]

Men: [*In the silences of the preceding conversation*]

What an intriguing woman. All those books. Those sleepless nights in the Residency in the Delta...

Yes... What can be behind that sweetness...?

Nearly every smile is enough to break your heart...

[*Silence*]

Anne-Marie Stretter: One might say practically nothing is... one can do practically nothing in India...

Young Attaché: [*Gentle*] You mean...?

Anne-Marie Stretter: Oh... nothing... the general despondency... [*There is a smile in her voice*].

Men and women:

They say she sometimes has bad ... attacks...

[*Low*] You mean... the trip to Chandernagor?

Yes. And something else... Sometimes she shuts herself up in her room... No one can see her...

Except him. Michael Richardson...

Yes, of course...

Anne-Marie Stretter: It's neither painful nor pleasant living in India. Neither easy nor difficult. It's nothing, really... nothing...

Young Attaché: [*Pause*] You mean it's impossible?

Anne-Marie Stretter: Well...[*Charming frivolity in her voice*]... yes... perhaps...[*Smile in her voice*] But that's probably an over-simplification...

Men and women:

She used to give concerts in Venice... She was one of the hopes of European music.

Was she very young when she left Venice?

Yes. She went away with a French civil servant that she left for Stretter.

[*Silence*]

Young Attaché: They say you're a Venetian.

Anne-Marie Stretter: My father was French. My mother... yes, she was from Venice.

[*Silence*]

Men and women: [*Continued*]

She plays nearly every evening. In the dry season, that is. [*Pause*] During the monsoon it's so damp pianos get out of tune overnight.

[*Silence*]

Young Attaché: The first time I saw you I thought you were English.

Anne-Marie Stretter: That does sometimes happen.

[*Pause*]

Young Attaché: Are there any who never get used to it?

Anne-Marie Stretter: [*Slowly*] Nearly everyone gets used to it.

[*Silence*]

Young Attaché: [*Suddenly crisp*] The French Vice-Consul in Lahore is looking at you.

[*No answer*]

Young Attaché: He's been looking at you all evening.

[*No answer*]

Young Attaché: Haven't you noticed?

[*She avoids answering*]

Anne-Marie Stretter: Where is he hoping to be posted, do you know?

Young Attaché: [*He knows*] Here in Calcutta.

Anne-Marie Stretter: Really...

Young Attaché: I imagined you knew.

[*No answer*]

[*Silence*]

[*Servants pass through. Dances follow one another; blues, tangos foxtrots*]

Anne-Marie Stretter: Did my husband tell you? We'd like to invite you to the islands.

Young Attaché: I'll be very pleased to come.

[*Silence*]

Man and woman:

If you listen closely, the voice has certain Italian inflexions...

[*Pause*]

Yes... Perhaps it's that... the foreign origin... that makes her seem... far away?

Perhaps...

Anne-Marie Stretter: You write, I believe?

Young Attaché: [*Pause*] I once thought I could. Before [*Pause*] Did someone tell you?

Anne-Marie Stretter: Yes, but I'd probably have guessed... [*Smile in the voice*] From your way of being silent...

Young Attaché: [*Smiling*] I gave it up. [*Pause*] Monsieur Stretter used to write too?

Anne-Marie Stretter: Yes, it did happen, to him too. And then... [*She stops*]

Young Attaché: [*Pause*] And you?

Anne-Marie Stretter: I've never tried...

Young Attaché: [*Crisply*] You think it's not worth it, don't you...?

Anne-Marie Stretter: [*Smile*] Well... [*She stops*] Well, yes, if you like...

[*Pause*]

Young Attaché: You play.

Anne-Marie Stretter: Sometimes. [*Pause*] Not so much, the last few years...

Young Attaché: [*Gently; love already*] Why?

Anne-Marie Stretter: [*Slowly*] It's hard to put it into words...

[*Long Pause*]

Young Attaché: Tell me.

Anne-Marie Stretter: For me.. for some time... there's been a kind of pain... associated with music...

[*No answer*]

[*Silence*]

[*The VICE-CONSUL moves from where he was standing in the garden and goes into the reception. The people still going back and forth between the garden and the reception watch him. A certain commotion. Some stifled exclamations. Then two or three couples come into the garden, as if they were running away from the man from Lahore*]

Women:

What's happening?

The Vice-Consul from Lahore has asked the wife of the First Secretary at the Spanish Embassy to dance...

[*Pause*]

Poor woman... but what are people afraid of?

They're not afraid... it's more a sort of repulsion... But it's...involuntary... you can't analyse it...

[*Silence*]

Young Attaché: Will you have to dance with him?

Anne-Marie Stretter: I don't have to do anything, but... [*Smile in the voice*]

[*Pause*]

Young Attaché: Last night he was in the garden. By the tennis courts.

[*The Answer comes slowly*]

Anne-Marie Stretter: I think he sleeps badly.

[*Pause*]

Young Attaché: He's still looking at you.

[*Silence*]

Isolated woman's voice:

> Poor woman... and on top of that she feels obliged to talk to him...

[*Silence*]

Young Attaché: Repulsion is a feeling you know nothing about?

[*Pause*]

Anne-Marie Stretter: I don't understand... How could one know nothing about it?

Young Attaché: [*Low*] The horror...

[*No answer*]

[*Silence*]

Young Attaché: [*Very clear and distinct*] They're talking about leprosy.

[*Silence*]

[*The YOUNG ATTACHÉ was referring to the conversation between the VICE-CONSUL and the wife (Spanish) of the Secretary at the Spanish Embassy*]

[*VICE-CONSUL and SPANISH WOMAN*]

Spanish Woman: [*Accent*]... the wife of one of our secretaries was going mad, thinking she'd caught it... impossible to get the idea out of her head.. she had to be sent back to Madrid...

Vice-Consul: She had leprosy?

Spanish Woman: [*Astonished*] Of course not!... accidents are very rare... in three years I only know of a ballboy at the Club... all the staff are examined regularly... most thorough.. I shouldn't have mentioned it... I don't know how it happened...

Vice-Consul: But I'm not frightened of leprosy.

Spanish Woman: Just as well, because... of course, there are worse places... Take Singapore...

Vice-Consul: [*Interrupting*] Don't you understand? I want to catch it.

[*Slight commotion*]

[*Then silence*]

Man and woman:

> She left him in the middle of the dance... What happened?
>
> He must have said something... something that frightened her.

[*Silence*]

[*Some guests leave the garden and go back into the reception. The BEGGAR sticks her bald head out and watches - like an owl. Then hides again. The YOUNG ATTACHÉ must have seen her*]

Young Attaché: There's a beggar woman in the garden.

Anne-Marie Stretter: I know... She's the one who sings - didn't you know? Of course, you've only just arrived in Calcutta... I think she sings a song from Savannakhet... That's in Laos... She intrigues us... I tell myself I must be mistaken, it's not possible, we're thousands of miles from Indochina here. How could she have done it?

Young Attaché: [*Pause*] I've heard her in the street, early in the morning... It's a cheerful song.

Anne-Marie Stretter: The children sing it in Laos... She must have come down through the river valley. But how did she cross the mountains - the Cardamom Hills?

Young Attaché: She's quite mad.

Anne-Marie Stretter: Yes, but you see... she's alive. Sometimes she comes to the islands. How? No one knows.

Young Attaché: Perhaps she follows you. Follows white people?

Anne-Marie Stretter: That happens. Food.

[*Some guests leave the reception. Slight fear*]

Men and women:

> Where is he?
>
> Over by the bar... He drinks too much, that fellow. It'll end badly.
>
> There's something... impossible... about him.
>
> Yes.
>
> And no one invited him anywhere in Lahore either?
>
> No.
>
> He went through hell in Lahore.
>
> Yes, but... How can one overcome this... this disgust...?

Men:

> He's anger personified.
>
> Against whom? Against what?

[*No answer*]

[*Silence*]

Women:

> He used to call down death on Lahore, fire and death.
>
> Perhaps he drank?
>
> No. no... Out here, drinking affects us all in the same way - we talk about going home... No, he wasn't drunk...

[*Two women come into the room. They are hot, they fan themselves. They look around. A blues. They look at the reception. Suddenly they stop fanning themselves: they've just seen something*]

[*Blues*]

Isolated woman's voice:

> It was bound to happen. Look... The Vice-Consul from Lahore is going over to Madame Stretter...

[*Silence*]

Men:

> Have you noticed? Out here the white people talk about nothing but themselves... The rest. And yet the time when most Europeans commit suicide is during famines...
>
> ... Which don't cause them any suffering...[*Little laugh*]
>
> No.

[*Silence*]

[*The two women watch with intense curiosity as the VICE-CONSUL goes over towards MADAME STRETTER. The sound of the reception ceases almost completely for a few seconds. Then it begins again, faintly. Politely stifled exclamations*]

Men and women: [*Conversations 1 and 2*]

No. 1:

> Did you see? The Ambassador...? How cleverly he got his wife out of it...

[*Silence*]

> Where are they going?
>
> Into the other drawing-room... of course, the Ambassador would have had to talk to him sooner or later... so...

[*Silence*]

No. 2:

Did you see? What diplomacy... everyone saw.

Where are they going?

Into the other drawing-room...[*Pause*] A servant's bringing them some champagne...

[*Silence*]

No. 1:

Why doesn't he go? Asking to be humiliated like that...

No. 2:

He said something to the Club Secretary that keeps coming back to me... "At home, in Neuilly, in a drawing-room, there's a big black piano - closed... On the music rest there's the score of *India Song*. My mother used to play it. I could hear it from my bedroom. It's been there ever since she died... "

What is it you find so striking?

The image.

[*Silence. Blues. MADAME STRETTER and the YOUNG ATTACHÉ are walking through the gardens*]

[*AMBASSADOR and VICE-CONSUL*]

Ambassador: If I've got it right, my dear fellow, you'd prefer Bombay? But you wouldn't be given the same job there as you had in [*He hesitates*] Lahore. It's too soon yet... Whereas if you stay here... people will forget... India is a gulf of indifference, really... if you like, I'll keep you on in Calcutta... Would you like me to?

Vice-Consul: Yes.

[*Silence*]

Women: [*Low*]

He told her he wanted to catch leprosy.

Mad...

[*Silence*]

Ambassador: Funny things, careers. The more you want one the less you make one. You can't just make a career. There are a thousand different ways of being a French Vice-Consul... If you forget Lahore other people will forget it too...

Vice-Consul: [*Pause*] I don't forget Lahore.

[*Silence*]

Isolated man's voice:

Only one person has anything to do with him. The Secretary at the European Club. A drunk.

Ambassador: You can't get used to Calcutta? [*No answer*] People put that sort of thing down to their nerves. There are remedies, you know.

Vice-Consul: No.

[*Silence*]

Woman and man: [*Low*]

And what are they taking about?

The reformatory in Arras. Childhood. And...[*Stops*]

And...

Her... the French Ambassador's wife...

[*Silence*]

Ambassador: At first everyone's like that. I remember I was, myself. You either go home or you stay. If you stay, you have to find...or rather invent... a way of looking at things... of enduring Lahore...

Vice-Consul: I couldn't.

[*Silence*]

Isolated woman's voice: [*Low*]

She's gone into the garden with the Young Attaché. [*Pause*] I told you.

[*Silence*]

Ambassador: Take my advice... weigh up the pros and cons... and if you're not... sure of yourself, go back to Paris...

Vice-Consul: No.

[*Silence*]

Ambassador: In that case... how do you see the future?

Vice-Consul: I see nothing.

[*Silence*]

Women: [*Low*]

After every reception the left-overs are given to the poor. Her idea. [*Lower*] She's coming back...

[*Silence*]

Oh, I see! The garden's full of beggars... crowds of them all round the kitchens...

The sentries have been told to let them through.

[*Silence*]

[*ANNE-MARIE STRETTER and the YOUNG ATTACHÉ come in again (from the left). They go towards the reception. The blues is over. Another takes up the theme of* India Song. *Before entering the reception ANNE-MARIE STRETTER halts, as does the YOUNG ATTACHÉ. They wait. For there, on the other side of the room, is the man from Lahore. Distraught, he comes towards her. Stops. Bows. Pale. The YOUNG ATTACHÉ makes a gesture as if to stop ANNE-MARIE STRETTER from accepting. She hesitates, but only for a second, and then accepts the man from Lahore's invitation to dance.* India Song *becomes very distant. All conversations grow faint, become intermittent murmurs. Almost total silence. At first, the VICE-CONSUL and ANNE-MARIE STRETTER dance in the room. The YOUNG ATTACHÉ watches them. Then they move towards the reception. The YOUNG ATTACHÉ moves forward, still watching them. Other people move towards the garden. They all look towards the reception*]

[*Conversation between ANNE-MARIE STRETTER and the VICE-CONSUL, low but violent, very slow*]

Vice-Consul: I didn't know that you existed.

[*No answer*]

Vice-Consul: Calcutta has become a form of hope for me.

[*Silence*]

Anne-Marie Stretter: I love Michael Richardson. I'm not free of that love.

Vice-Consul: I know. I love you like that, in that love. It doesn't matter to me.

[*No answer*]

Vice-Consul: My voice sounds odd. Can you hear? It frightens them.

Anne-Marie Stretter: Yes.

Vice-Consul: Whose voice is it?

[*No answer*]

Vice-Consul: I shot at myself in Lahore, but I didn't die. Other people separate me from Lahore. I don't separate myself. Lahore is me. Do you understand too?

[*Pause*]

Anne-Marie Stretter: [*Gently*] Yes. Don't shout.

Vice-Consul: No.

[*Silence*]

Vice-Consul: You are with me about Lahore. I know. You are in me. I'll carry you inside me. [*Terrible brief laugh*] And you'll shoot the Shalimar lepers with me. What can you do about it?

[*Silence*]

Vice-Consul: I didn't need to dance with you to know you. You know that.

Anne-Marie Stretter: Yes.

[*Pause*]

Vice-Consul: There's no need for us to go any further, you and I. [*Terrible brief laugh*] We haven't anything to say to each other. We are the same.

[*Pause*]

Anne-Marie Stretter: I believe you.

[*Pause*]

Vice-Consul: Love affairs you have with others. We don't need that.

[*Silence*]

[*The VICE-CONSUL's voice is broken by a sob. It is no longer under his control*]

Vice-Consul: I wanted to know the smell of your hair - that's why I... [*He stops. A sob*]

[*Silence*]

[*His voice returns to normal - almost*]

Vice-Consul: After the reception your friends stay on. I'd like to stay with you for once.

Anne-Marie Stretter: You haven't a chance.

[*Pause*]

Vice-Consul: They'd throw me out.

Anne-Marie Stretter: Yes. You're someone they have to forget.

[*Pause*]

Vice-Consul: Like Lahore.

Anne-Marie Stretter: Yes.

[*Silence*]

Vice-Consul: What will become of me?

Anne-Marie Stretter: You'll be posted somewhere a long way from Calcutta.

[*Pause*]

Vice-Consul: That's what you want.

Anne-Marie Stretter: Yes.

[*Pause*]

Vice-Consul: Very well. And when will it end?

Anne-Marie Stretter: When you die, I believe.

[*Silence*]

Vice-Consul: [*Heartrending*] What's this pain? Mine?

[*Pause*]

Anne-Marie Stretter: Knowledge.

Vice-Consul: [*Terrible laugh*] Of you?

[*No answer*]

[*Silence*]

Vice-Consul: I'm going to shout. I'm going to ask them to let me stay tonight.

[*Pause*]

Anne-Marie Stretter: [*Pause*] Do as you like.

Vice-Consul: So that something should happen between us. In public. Shouting is all I know. Let them at least find out a love can be shouted.

[*No answer*]

Vice-Consul: They'll feel uncomfortable for half an hour. Then they'll start talking again.

[*No answer*]

Vice-Consul: I even know you won't tell anyone you agreed.

[*No answer*]

[*Silence*]

[India Song *ends. It is replaced by "Heure Exquise", sung. The sky grows pale. Two men, drunk, stagger in and collapse into armchairs. Over "Heure Exquise", mingled with it, the VICE-CONSUL's first cry*]

Vice-Consul: Let me stay!

[*Silence*]

[*Guests shrink back towards the garden. The two drunk men laugh. The others are horrified*]

Vice-Consul: I'm going to stay here tonight, with her, for once, with her! Do you hear?

[*Silence*]

Isolated woman's voice:

How awful...

Isolated voice of young Attaché:

You really ought to go home, you've had too much to drink... come along...

[*"Heure Exquise" still. The VICE-CONSUL shrieks*]

Vice-Consul: I'm going to stay! In the French Embassy! I'm going to the islands with her! Please! Please! Let me stay!

[*Silence*]

Isolated woman's voice: [*Anguished*]

She looks as if she didn't hear...

Another: [*The same*]

This is terrible....

[*Silence*]

Vice-Consul: [*Shrieking*] Once! Just once! I've never loved anyone but her!

[*Silence*]

Isolated man's voice: [To *VICE-CONSUL*]

We're sorry, but you're the sort of person who only interests us when you're not there.

[*Silence*]

Isolated woman's voice:

How cruel... It's terrible... horrible...

[*The VICE-CONSUL's sobs, unrestrained. All dignity swept away. Everyone suddenly turns aside*]

Isolated woman's voice:

I can't bear to see it...

[*The VICE-CONSUL appears, shaken with sobs. We see and hear them. A man and a stranger, leads him by the arm towards the entrance of the Embassy. The VICE-CONSUL resists at first, then lets himself be led away. They disappear. Everyone stands looking after them*]

Isolated woman's voice:

He's gone. [*Long Pause*] They're shutting the gate.

[*In the distance, the same cries: the VICE-CONSUL has started to shout again*]

Isolated woman's voice:

He was laughing and crying at the same time. Did you see?

[*Silence*]

[*"Heure Exquise" continues imperturbably to the end, while everyone stands looking away from the reception and towards the VICE-CONSUL. The cries still go on*]

Isolated man's voice:

He's trying to break down the gate.

[*Silence*]

[*"Heure Exquise" ends. The cries get farther away*]

Isolated voice:

The beggars are frightened...

Isolated voice: [*The last*]

He's gone.

[*Silence. A few seconds of it, then:*]

[*Blackout*]

[*Darkness gradually blots out the picture as, in the far distance, the silhouette of the beggar woman passes by, then disappears*]

[*Silence*]

[*Then suddenly, on the piano, Beethoven's 14th Variation on a Theme of Diabelli*]

[*Blackout*]

III

We are in the same part of the Embassy as before. There are five people there in the darkness, which slowly disappears: ANNE-MARIE STRETTER, MICHAEL RICHARDSON, the YOUNG ATTACHÉ, the GUEST (friend of the Stretters') and an old friend, and Englishman, GEORGE CRAWN.

The drunk journalists have gone. The rest are by themselves, in an intimacy in which each of them feels alone. It is late, they are separated by fatigue.

They are waiting. Their chairs - except for those of ANNE-MARIE STRETTER and MICHAEL RICHARDSON - are too far apart for conversation. The YOUNG ATTACHÉ and the Stretters' GUEST look exhausted, also by the events of the evening.

We don't know what they are waiting for: perhaps for it to be light, so that they can leave for the islands. Probably. We still hear Beethoven's 14th Variation on a Theme by Diabelli. Through the music, the sounds of Calcutta grow stronger with the light.

ANNE-MARIE STRETTER sits with her head flung back and to one side over the arm of a chair. She might seem to be asleep if it weren't for the fact that her eyes are open. MICHAEL RICHARDSON is near her, half lying on a low chair.

The YOUNG ATTACHÉ is sitting up straight, smoking. He looks as if he is listening to the noises of Calcutta, through which one suddenly recognises the cries, the last spasms of the calls to love of the VICE-CONSUL from Lahore. The YOUNG ATTACHÉ obviously finds them hard to bear. The others do not.

The Stretters' GUEST, standing, looks around at the others: these people of India whom he thought he knew, but whom he scarcely recognises after the night of the reception. He too listens to the cries of the VICE-CONSUL.

GEORGE CRAWN listens to the Beethoven: he is entirely absorbed by the music.

[See notes on Voices 3 and 4 on page 121]

Voice 4: As usual after a reception, some people stayed on.

Voice 3: [*Low*] Is he the one sitting near her - Michael Richardson?

Voice 4: Yes. 0

Voice 3: Did they ever find out...?

Voice 4: [*Hesitating*] After she died he left India.

[*Silence*]

Voice 4: [*Continuing*] The one standing up is the Young Attaché.

Voice 3: And the elderly Englishman?

Voice 4: George Crawn. He knew her in Peking.

[*Pause*]

Voice 3: And the one looking at them?

Voice 4: Someone passing through. Stretter's guest.

[*Silence*]

Voice 3: Is that the French Vice-Consul shouting?

Voice 4: Yes. Still.

[*Silence*]

Voice 4: All trace of him disappears in 1938. [*Pause*] He resigns from the consular service. The resignation is the last thing on the file.

Voice 3: [*Hesitating*] Very soon afterwards....

Voice 4: A few days.

[*Silence. Cries*]

Voice 3: What's he shouting?

Voice 4: Her name.

[*Pause*]

Voice 3: [*Slowly*] Anna Maria Guardi.

Voice 4: Yes. All night, all through Calcutta, he's been shouting that name.

[*Silence*]

[*The women's voices (from Act One) now arrive. They too speak of the VICE-CONSUL*]

Voice 2: [*As is exhausted*] He walks along by the Ganges. He comes on the lepers asleep. Someone else is shouting on the other bank.

[*Pause*]

Voice 1: Yes.

[*Silence*]

Voice 2: Can you see him?

Voice 1: [*Distant*] Yes. I'm watching. I see.

[*Silence*]

Voice 2: [*Slow*] Is he looking for something?... Or walking at random?... Aimlessly?

[*No Answer*]

Voice 2: Is he looking for something he's lost?

[*No answer*]

Voice 2: Something in common that he's lost too?

[*No answer*]

Voice 2: The love of her?

Voice 1: Love. Yes.

[*Silence*]

Voice 2: [*Yearning, desire*] How far away you are... from me...

[*No answer*]

[*Silence*]

[*A servant goes through with trays piled with glasses, ashtrays, etc. He passes them as though he didn't see them. Gleams in the sky. The burning-ghats*]

Voice 1: [*Slow*] It will soon be day.

[*Silence*]

Voice 1: [*Very slow*] Dawn is breaking here, all round. And there. The air smells of mud. And leprosy. And burning.

Voice 2: Not a breath.

Voice 1: Slow stirrings, slow movements, smells.

[*Silence*]

Voice 2: Can't I hear music?

Voice 1: No.

Voice 2: That sound of wings, of birds.

Voice 1: The fan. Forgotten.

[*Silence*]

[*The men's voices mingle with the women's*]

Voice 3: Those gleams.

Voice 4: Day. The first zone is the zone of leprosy and dogs. They are on the banks of the Ganges, under the trees. No strength left. No pain.

Voice 3: And those who have died of hunger?

Voice 4: Farther away, in the density of the North. The last zone.

[*Pause*]

Voice 4: Day. The sun.

[*Pause*]

Voice 3: The light. Terrible

[*Silence*]

Voice 1: The light. Of exile.

Voice 2: Is she asleep?

Voice 1: Which one?

Voice 2: The white woman.

Voice 1: No. Resting.

[*Silence*]

Voice 2: [*Mournfully*] How far away you are. Quite absent.

[*No answer*]

[*Silence*]

[*MICHAEL RICHARDSON slowly turns his head towards ANNE-MARIE STRETTER. Looks at her*]

Voice 3: [*Startled*] Voices near us suddenly? Did you hear?

Voice 4: [*Pause*] No...

Voice 3: Young voices... women's?

Voice 4: [*Pause*] I don't hear anything. [*Pause*] Silence.

[*Silence*]

Voice 4: He's looking at her.

Voice 3: Yes. She is far away. Quite absent.

[*Silence*]

Voice 4: [*In one breath*] People said one day they'd both be found dead in a brothel in Calcutta they used to go to sometimes during the monsoon.

[*Silence*]

Voice 3: Not a breath. The heat is the colour of rust. Above, the smoke.

Voice 4: The factories. The Middle zone.

[*Silence*]

[*Very slowly ANNE-MARIE STRETTER has inclined her head towards MICHAEL RICHARDSON. They look at each other*]

Voice 3: That overhanging mass...?

Voice 4: The monsoon. Below, Bengal.

Voice 3: And farther away... lower... under the clouds...? Look...

[*No answer*]

Voice 3: That white patch... in a bend in the Ganges...? There?...

Voice 4: [*Hesitating*] The English cemetery.

[*Silence*]

[*The stranger and the YOUNG ATTACHÉ begin to look at ANNE-MARIE STRETTER*]

Voice 1: Is she a leper?

Voice 2: Which one?

Voice 1: The beggar.

Voice 2: She sleeps in leprosy, and every morning... No. [*Pause*] No.

[*Silence*]

Voice 1: And the white woman?

Voice 2: A false alarm ten years ago. But no, neither. [*Pause*] Listen....

[*Sound of a machine and of water*]

Voice 1: The water-sprinklers in the English quarter.

[*Silence*]

[*The men turn their eyes from ANNE-MARIE STRETTER and look at the ground. The stage gradually gets lighter*]

Voice 1: A car is speeding along the straight roads. Beside the Ganges.

Voice 2: Black?

Voice 1: Yes.

Voice 2: They've left for the islands.

[*Silence*]

[*The fires of the ghats are out. It is day-light. Pale day-light. They lie there, in the same deathly attitude, as the voices describe the journey*]

Voice 4: The French Embassy black Lancia has started out for the Delta.

[*Long silence*]

Voice 3: [*As if reciting a lesson*] The granary of northern India... The frontier of the waters. The Delta.

Voice 4: Yes, mingling of the waters. The sweet and the salt.

Voice 3: After the deluge, before the light...

[*Pause*]

Voice 3: And those junks?

Voice 4: Rice. Sailing down to Coromandel.

[*Pause*]

Voice 3: Those dark patches on the banks?

Voice 4: People. The highest density in the world.

[*Silence*]

Voice 3: Those thousands of dark mirrors?

Voice 4: The paddy fields of India.

[*Silence*]

Voice 4: They're asleep. She's lying close to him.

[*Silence*]

Voice 3: She used to wake up late during the monsoon?

Voice 4: Yes. Didn't go out till after dark.

[*Silence*]

Voice 3: The black Lancia has stopped.

Voice 4: The rain. The roads are blocked. They took shelter in a rest-house. [*As if reading*] It was there the Young Attaché said: "I saw the Vice-Consul again before I left. He was still shouting in the streets. He asked me if I was going to the islands. I said no, I was going to Nepal with the Ambassador."

[*Pause*]

Voice 3: Did she approve of the Young Attaché's lie?

Voice 4: She practically never mentioned the man from Lahore.

[*Silence*]

Voice 3: That patch of green? It's getting bigger...

Voice 4: The sea.

[*Silence*]

[*Blackout*]

[*The voices speak in the dark*]

Voice 4: The islands.

Voice 3: Which one?

Voice 4: The biggest, the middle one. They're there.

[*Silence*]

Voice 3: That big white building....?

Voice 4: A big international hotel. The Prince of Wales. The sea is rough. There's been a storm.

[*Blackout ends*]

IV

The same as before, but it has become a lounge in the Prince of Wales. They are not there. A bright, greenish light instead of that of the monsoon. Two servants in white gloves are putting up green canvas blinds over the screened windows. We do not recognise the garden. It has exploded into a violent green light - the garden of the Prince of Wales. All that remains of the garden in Calcutta are some clumps of foliage.

The sound of the sea gradually spreads, increasing every second, until it invades everything. Then it remains stable.

The wind makes the blinds flap.

Sound of launches' sirens in the distance.

Close, the cheeping of birds.

The fan is still there, going round at the same nightmare slow speed.

In the distance, a dance: an orchestra is playing India Song.

The sounds occur one after the other, e.g.:

> *The wind.*
>
> *The sea.*
>
> *Sirens.*
>
> *Birds.*
>
> *Dance.*

As the two servants put up the blinds, thus creating the set for the Prince of Wales, VOICES 3 and 4 speak at each other.

VOICE 4 remains the same throughout.

VOICE 3 changes as the end of the story approaches. It becomes either more pressing or, conversely, less eager to question. When it speaks of ANNE-MARIE STRETTER it gets lower, with silences between words and phrases.

Voice 4: In front, the landing stages. The boats go to and from the South Pacific. Behind, there's a yachting harbour.

[*Silence*]

Voice 3: Beyond the palms, the same flat horizon.

Voice 4: They're alluvial islands, formed by the Ganges mud.

[*Silence*]

Voice 3: Where's the French residency?

Voice 4: The other side of the hotel, looking out to sea.

[*The servants go out. They have "finished" the set for the Prince of Wales. When they have gone the sound of the dance is heard in the distance. They are playing* India Song]

Voice 4: At this time of the day, people used to start to drink at all the tables in the Prince of Wales. On the sideboards there are French grapes. In the showcase, perfumes. Roses are sent every day from Nepal.

Voice 3: Who lives in this hotel?

Voice 4: White India.

[*Silence*]

Voice 3: [*Almost shouting*] What's that sudden smell of death?

Voice 4: Incense.

[*The smell of incense should pervade the auditorium*]

[*Silence*]

Voice 3: She wanted to go for a swim when they got here?

Voice 4: Yes. It was late, the sea was rough, it was impossible to swim. Just let the waves break over you. She and he both went in.

[*Silence*]

Voice 3: [*Afraid*] All those screens in the sea?

Voice 4: Protection against the sharks.

Voice 3: Oh.

[*Silence*]

Voice 3: Where is she?

Voice 4: She'll come.

[*Silence*]

Voice 4: Here she is.

Voice 3: [*Hesitating; lower, more slowly*] Was she like that that night...?

Voice 4: Smiling. Dressed in white.

[*Silence*]

[*These last two phrases should be felt as terrifying: ANNE-MARIE STRETTER's smile, the whiteness of her dress. In the green light, ANNE-MARIE STRETTER enters. Smiling, dressed in white*]

[*She goes and looks at the sea, beyond the garden. The four men enter, also dressed in white, from different parts of the hotel. They all go towards the garden and look out at the sea. MICHAEL RICHARDSON turns and gazes at ANNE-MARIE STRETTER. She doesn't look at him any more. In the distance, a voice over a loudspeaker*]

Loudspeaker: The last boat tonight leaves at seven o'clock.

Voice 4: That's for the tourists who want to get back. There's a storm threatening.

[*Ships' sirens. Then silence*]

Voice 4: The last launch has just arrived. The one that brings supplies.

[*Silence*]

[*A head waiter comes and bows to the five people. Their table is ready. They go off towards the left. Still the distant airport music*]

Voice 4: [*Pause*] Their table's ready. The food here is excellent. Michael Richardson used to say that once you knew the Prince of Wales you were never really satisfied anywhere else in the world.

Voice 3: [*Low*] I can't quite remember... isn't she going to the French residency?

Voice 4: She only used to sleep there. She used to dine at the Prince of Wales when she stayed on the islands. [*Hesitates*] She'd had the servants at the Residency sent back to Calcutta.

[*Pause*]

[*Fear*]

Voice 3: [*Low*] How long ago?

Voice 4: A few weeks.

[*Bird cries, so loud they are almost unbearable*]

Voice 3: The birds... thousands of them.

Voice 4: Prisoners on the islands. They couldn't fly back to the coast because of the storm.

Voice 3: It's as if they were right inside the hotel...

Voice 4: They're in the mango trees. They strip them. They'll fly away when it's light.

[*Noise of birds swamps everything else*]

[*Silence*]

Voice 3: There's dancing at the other end of the lounge.

Voice 4: Tourists from Ceylon.

[*Silence*]

Voice 4: During dinner... she asked them to raise the blind. She wants to see the sea, the sky, above the estuaries. They scarcely speak, they're tired from last night.

[*Silence*]

Voice 3: She's not eating anything.

Voice 4: Hardly anything. She's looking out of the window.

Voice 3: I remember... A wall of mist is sweeping towards the islands.

Voice 4: Yes. She's saying something about Venice. [*Effort of memory*] Venice in the winter... yes, that's right....

[*Pause*]

Voice 3: Venice...

Voice 4: Yes. Perhaps, some winter evenings in Venice, the same kind of mist...

Voice 3: ... she's saying the name of... [*Stops*] of a colour...

Voice 4: Purple. The colour of the mist in the Delta...

[*Silence*]

[*Beyond the green windows of the hotel, dishevelled, exhausted, his features contorted, still wearing his white dinner jacket, appears the French VICE-CONSUL. He goes through the garden of the hotel, searching. Disappears. Then reappers almost at once on the stage, now the lounge of the Prince of Wales, walks across the room, looks towards the left, stops short. He has seen her. He stands there looking at her*]

Voice 3: He came over by the last boat.

Voice 4: Yes. The seven o'clock.

[*Pause*]

He hadn't been home all day. [*Pause*] He never went back to Calcutta.

[*Silence*]

[*The tune of* India Song *is played loudly for a few seconds, then fades*]

Voice 3: India Song...

Voice 4: Yes.

[*Silence*]

Voice 4: Now that the mist has come the wind has dropped.

[*Silence*]

[*Some tourists go by in the garden beyond the green windows. One can make out women fanning themselves with white fans. Light-coloured dresses*]

Voice 4: They're talking about the beggar woman.

[*No answer*]

[*Silence*]

Voice 4: George Crawn and the Stretters' guest are talking about the beggar woman.

[*Silence*]

FIRST VERSION

[*The conversation between GEORGE CRAWN and the Stretters' GUEST is heard as from some distance. (Very light and ordinary)*]

George Crawn: She doesn't know a word of Hindustani.

Guest: Not a word. If she's from Savannakhet she must have come through Laos, Cambodia, Siam and Burma, and then probably down through the Irrawaddy Valley... Mandalay... Prome... Bassein...

George Crawn: It must have been not just one journey, as we might think, but hundreds, thousands, every day, each one the last... hunger always driving her on, farther and farther... she must have followed roads, railways, boats... but what's strange is that she always went towards the sunset...

Guest: ...I suppose she travelled at night, and faced towards the light... she's bald... because of hunger, do you think?

George Crawn: Yes.

[*Pause*]

George Crawn: Sometimes she comes to the islands. Following the whites, probably: food... In Calcutta she lives by the Ganges, under the trees. She gets up at night and goes through the English quarter. Apparently she hunts for food at night along the Ganges.

[*Pause*]

Guest: And what's left of her in Calcutta? Not much... The song of Savannakhet, the laugh... and her native language is still there of course, but there's no use for it. The madness was there when she arrived... already too far gone...

[*Pause*]

George Crawn: Why Calcutta? Why did her journey stop there?

Guest: Perhaps because she can lose herself there. She's always been trying to lose herself, really, ever since her life began...

[*Pause*]

George Crawn: She too.

Guest: Yes...

[*Silence*]

SECOND VERSION

[*VOICES 3 AND 4 relate the conversation between GEORGE CRAWN and the Stretters' GUEST (VOICE 4 is the one that hears it)*]

Voice 4: They've seen her. She must have crossed the Delta on the roof of a bus. She stowed away on the last boat. They met her by the lagoon, a few hundred yards from the French Residency.

[*Pause*]

Voice 3: She must have been following Anne-Marie Stretter....

Voice 4: The guest says she followed him to the gate. She frightened him. He said: "That eternal smile is frightening"...

Voice 3: That too....

Voice 4: Yes. [*Pause*] You remember? The first attempt... [*Stops*] at Savannakhet, because of a dead child....

Voice 3: ...Sold by its mother, a beggar from the North... very young....?

Voice 4: Yes. Seventeen....[*Pause*] A few days before Stretter arrived.

[*Silence*]

[*Suddenly the VICE-CONSUL goes towards the right, and disappears: he has seen them. Here they are, coming out from dinner. There are now only three of them: ANNE-MARIE STRETTER, MICHAEL RICHARDSON, the YOUNG ATTACHÉ. They walk across the lounge, making for the garden through the middle door. In the garden they separate. ANNE-MARIE STRETTER goes to the right. The others go straight on through the garden and disappear. The VICE-CONSUL begins to go after ANNE-MARIE STRETTER. He halts. She has stopped too. She looks round her to the sea, the palms. She hasn't seen the VICE-CONSUL*]

Voice 4: She wanted to walk back on her own.

[*Silence*]

Voice 4: The other two went for a sail...

[*Silence*]

Voice 4: The Young Attaché and Michael Richardson went back to the French Residency the other way along the beach.

[*Pause*]

Voice 4: It was as hot again as it had been in Calcutta.

[*ANNE-MARIE STRETTER walks slowly away. Behind her, the VICE-CONSUL. He is following her. They disappear*]

[*Blackout*]

[*During the blackout, the 14th Beethoven-Diabelli Variation in the distance*]

[*Blackout fades*]

V

The same as before, but it is now the French Residency. The light is different. It seems to come from outside. It is blue, like moonlight.

The fan is still there. Still going round.

The garden of the Embassy and the garden of the hotel have both gone. There is just an empty space. A path, and at the end of it a white gate.

Everything is enveloped in endless, fathomless emptiness. But it has a sound: the sea.

After a while, MICHAEL RICHARDSON and the YOUNG ATTACHÉ come in through the white gate.

Simultaneously, she enters, from the left of the house. She is barefoot. Her hair is loose. She wears the short black cotton wrap. She joins them on the path, they go towards one another, meet in the half-light. They look at the sea.

Voice 4: She's supposed to have said she was worried about George Crawn and the Guest. The sea was rough.

[*Sound of a rowing boat in the distance. They all look towards something out at sea*]

Voice 4: She didn't have to worry any more. George Crawn and the Guest went straight back to the hotel without calling in at the Residency.

[*Silence*]

[*They slowly walk back into the house*]

Voice 3: [*Pause; stricken*] She didn't say anything that evening that might have made anyone think... [*Stops*]

Voice 4: No. Nothing.

[*Terrific tension. But nothing breaks the quiet spell of death. MICHAEL RICHARDSON goes over to the piano. She goes out of the room. The two men are left alone. They look at each other. Outside, in the distance, at the end of the path, the white shape of the VICE-CONSUL comes through the open gate. They don't see him. She comes back, bringing glasses and champagne. She smiles at them. She puts the bottle and glasses down on a low table and pours out the champagne. She takes it to them. They drink. She sits down on a sofa. There is still the fixed smile on ANNE-MARIE STRETTER'S face. Outside the VICE-CONSUL watches. MICHAEL RICHARDSON plays]*

[He plays the 14th Beethoven-Diabelli Variation. Complete stillness]

[Suddenly the stillness is shattered. the YOUNG ATTACHÉ goes over to ANNE-MARIE STRETTER, puts his arms round her, then falls at her feet, and stays there with his arms round her legs]

[He stays there, rivetted to her. She doesn't prevent him. Strokes his hair. Still the smile. The fixed smile. He gets up. Draws her to her feet, flings his arms round her body, naked under the wrap. A gesture of supplication. Vain. They kiss. A long kiss. MICHAEL RICHARDSON watches. Plays the piano and watches them. His face is as we have always known it. The white shape from Lahore gazes in avidly from outside. The YOUNG ATTACHÉ roughly releases ANNE-MARIE STRETTER, staggers over to the piano and leans on it with his head in his hands. The Beethoven continues: MICHAEL RICHARDSON goes on playing. Stillness. Stillness enveloped in music. The YOUNG ATTACHÉ remains leaning on the piano, motionless. The attitude of despair itself. For the last time, one of the women's voices]

Voice 2: [*Terrified*] Where are you? [*Waits. No Answer*] You're so far away...I'm frightened...

[VOICE 1 doesn't answer any more]

[Silence]

[ANNE-MARIE STRETTER turns towards the outside, towards the sea. Shows no surprise when she sees the VICE-CONSUL. He doesn't move, makes no attempt to conceal himself. Gazes fixedly at her. She turns and bares her body to the fan. Perhaps her naked body is visible to everyone]

[To the VICE-CONSUL also - the body already separate from her. She stands there motionless under the fan]

[Silence]

Voice 3: [*Low, almost a murmur*] Michael Richardson left her alone that evening?

Voice 4: [*Hesitating*] It has been agreed between the lovers of the Ganges that they'd leave each other free if ever either of them decided... [*Stops*]

[Silence]

Voice 3: [*Suffering, terror*] But he doesn't know, it isn't possible...

[*No answer*]

Voice 3: What does he know?

Voice 4: [*Pause*] Ever since the servants were sent away, Michael Richardson had been living with this possibility.

[*Silence*]

[*ANNE-MARIE STRETTER has lain under the fan. She has closed her eyes. MICHAEL RICHARDSON and the YOUNG ATTACHÉ slowly tear themselves away, as if she had actually ordered them to leave her alone there. They cross the empty space outside. Shadows. The VICE-CONSUL is there. He doesn't hide as they go past. It is as if they do not see him. They disapper from sight. ANNE-MARIE STRETTER and the VICE-CONSUL from Lahore are the only ones left in the French Residency*]

[*Silence*]

[*She gets up, goes out, slowly walks through the empty space towards the white gate. It is as if she doesn't see anything. She doesn't see the VICE-CONSUL. And he makes not the slightest gesture towards her*]

Voice 3: [*Scarcely breathed*] Is he the only one who saw...?

Voice 4: He didn't say.

Voice 3: [*As before*]... he didn't do anything to stop...

[*No answer*]

Voice 4: The Young Attaché came back to the Residency in the course of the night. He saw her. She was lying on the path, resting on her elbow. He said: "She laid her arm out straight and leaned her head on it. The Vice-Consul from Lahore was sitting ten yards away. They didn't speak to each other."

[*Silence*]

[*What has just been related is what ANNE-MARIE STRETTER does. She lays her face on her arm. Stay like that. The VICE-CONSUL looks at her, rivetted to the distance between them*]

Voice 4: She must have stayed there a long while, till daylight - and then she must have gone along the path... [*Stops*] They found the wrap on the beach.

[*Silence*]

[*The fan stops. Rest a few seconds on the stopping of the fan*]

[*Blackout*]

Summary

This summary is the only one which should accompany productions of *India Song*.

This is the story of a love affair which takes place in India in the thirties, in an overpopulated city on the banks of the Ganges. Two days in this love story are presented. It is the season of the summer monsoon.

Four voices - facelessly - speak of the story. Two of the voices are those of young women, two are men's.

The Voices do not address the spectator or reader, they are totally independent. They speak among themselves, and do not know they are being heard.

The Voices have known or read of this love story long ago. Some of them remember it better than others. But none of them remembers it completely. And none of them has completely forgotten it.

We never know who the Voices are. But just by the way each of them has forgotten or remembers, we get to know them more deeply than through their identity.

The story is a love story immobilized in the culmination of passion. Around it is another story, a story of horror - famine and leprosy mingled in the pestilential humidity of the monsoon - which is immobilized too in a daily paroxysm.

The woman, Anne-Marier Stretter, wife of a French Ambassador in India and now dead - her grave is in the English cemetery in Calcutta - might be said to be born of this horror. She stands in the midst of it with a grace which engulfs everything, in unfailing silence - a grace which the Voices try to see again, a grace which is porous and dangerous, dangerous also for some of them.

B e s i d e
the woman, in the same city, there is a man, the French Vice-Consul in Lahore, in Calcutta in disgrace. It is by anger and murder that he is connected to the horror of India.

There is a reception at the French Embassy, in the course of which the outcast Vice-Consul cries out his love to Anne-Marie Stretter, as white India looks on.

After the reception she drives along the straight roads of the Delta to the islands in the estuary.

THE END